FORT CONCHO

FORT CONCHO

A History and a Guide

By James T. Matthews

TEXAS STATE
HISTORICAL ASSOCIATION

Library of Congress Cataloging-in-Publication Data

Matthews, James T.
   Fort Concho: a history and a guide/ by James T. Matthews
    p.   cm.   —(The Fred Rider Cotten popular history series; no. 18)
   Includes bibliographical references.
   ISBN 0-87611-205-X (pbk. : alk. paper)
   1. Fort Concho (Tex.)—History. 2. Frontier and pioneer life—Texas—Concho
River Region. 3. Concho River Region (Tex.)—History. 4. Concho River Region
(Tex.)—History, Military. 5. United States. Army—Military life—History—19th
century. I. Title. II. Series.
  F394.F62M37   2005
  976.4'71—dc22   2005012473

Published by the Texas State Historical Association in cooperation with the Center
for Studies in Texas History at the University of Texas at Austin.

Cover: Reenactors keep the history of Fort Concho alive today. From front to back:
Rickey Rinehart (Tenth U.S. Cavalry, Memorial); Bob Broene (Third U.S. Artillery,
Memorial); and Shawn Pascuzzi (Fourth U.S. Cavalry, Memorial) in front of the
Headquarters Building at Fort Concho. *Courtesy Fort Concho Library and Archives.*

CONTENTS

In more than twenty years of federal service Fort Concho was home to companies of fifteen regiments in the regular United States Army. The post provided a focal point for major campaigns against the Comanches, Kiowas, and Apaches. Patrols from Fort Concho charted vast areas of West Texas and provided a climate for settlement on the Texas frontier. *Courtesy Fort Concho Library and Archives.*

1.
ON THE PLATEAU WHERE THE RIVERS JOIN: BUILDING FORT CONCHO

IN THE FALL OF 1867 the United States Army established a permanent camp on the plateau where the North and Middle Concho rivers join. For centuries, this high open plateau had remained barren except for passing expeditions or hunting parties. The Jumano Indians had established a village downstream on the North Concho by the 1530s, and Cabeza de Vaca stayed there on his way west in 1534. Almost a century later, between 1629 and 1632, a mission under the leadership of Franciscans Juan de Salas and Diego Lopez conducted Christian services at the thriving Jumano village. By the 1650s Spanish traders from Santa Fe became frequent visitors at the Concho River settlement. Some collected the conchos, or shells, for which the river was named and harvested them for pearls. Around 1690 the Jumanos abandoned the area entirely in the face of Apache advances onto the South Plains of Texas.[1]

In the mid 1700s the Apaches also moved on to the south and west as the Concho River country came under the control of Comanches, the fearless horsemen of the plains. The Comanche war trail crossed the Conchos on its way from Big Spring to the Rio Grande. As the flags of Spain, Mexico, the Republic of Texas, and finally the United States successively flew over the European settlements of Texas, the Comanches continued to travel freely across the South Plains. Then in 1849, following the war with Mexico,

American citizens began to cross West Texas. They came seeking trade routes and trails to the gold fields of California. The United States Army surveyed these routes and proposed that a line of outposts be established along the Comanche frontier to enforce peace through a strong military presence among the tribes. In March 1852 troops manned Camp Joseph E. Johnston, a temporary site on the North Concho River. It was abandoned with the founding of Fort Chadbourne on a tributary of the Colorado River in October 1852. Patrols from Fort Chadbourne scouted south along the Concho River throughout the 1850s. Lt. Col. Robert E. Lee led one of the scouting expeditions in the summer of 1856. In 1858 the short-lived Butterfield Overland Mail route crossed the North Concho and ran west along the Middle Concho on its way to the Horsehead Crossing on the Pecos River and then on to California.[2]

With the outbreak of the Civil War in 1861 United States troops surrendered all the frontier outposts in Texas to the Confederacy. In February 1861 Capt. Robert B. Halley's rangers from Bell County took command of Fort Chadbourne. Texas troops continued to man the post until the end of the war. The U.S. Army returned to Texas after the defeat of the Confederacy in 1865.

The army's initial efforts concentrated on administering Reconstruction and providing a show of force against the French government of Maximilian in Mexico. Yet a series of events rapidly altered the mission of Federal troops in Texas. The French withdrew from Mexico in the spring of 1867. By this time, Texans searching for a means of survival had already begun to herd cattle across the Concho river region. The Goodnight–Loving cattle trail followed the Middle Concho west in 1866. To protect the growing number of cattlemen and settlers in the Concho corridor, the Fourth United States Cavalry remanned Fort Chadbourne in May 1867. At the same time, the army made plans to locate a permanent outpost central to the area with a more reliable supply of water.[3]

During the summer of 1867 Maj. John P. Hatch, commander of the Fourth Cavalry, ordered Lt. Peter M. Boehm to establish a permanent camp on the Middle Concho River about fifty miles from Fort Chadbourne. The camp soon moved to the North Concho, where fifty troopers under Capt. Michael J. Kelly remained on

Maj. John P. Hatch. While he commanded Fort Concho in 1870, Hatch experimented with adobe as a substitute for limestone in some of the post buildings. Although the experiment failed, Hatch retained the nickname "Dobe." *Courtesy the National Archives.*

duty throughout the summer.[4] In September a board of officers including Major Hatch surveyed the North and Middle Concho rivers to determine a site for the permanent post. They chose the plateau at the junction of the rivers because of "the large quantity and quality of grass—the almost inexhaustible supply of limestone and rock and land for building and the large and never ending supply of good running water."[5]

On November 28, 1867, Company H, Fourth Cavalry, left Fort Chadbourne to establish a permanent garrison on the Concho. Capt. George G. Huntt named the new station Camp Hatch. He described the site as "close to all the watering places frequented by the Indians after crossing the plains." Unfortunately, he continued, "The country is but poorly timbered—mesquite on the land and straggling pecans along the streams." To insure a regular line of supply and building materials, construction began immediately on a wagon road from the new site to the San Saba River near Fort Mason. Huntt's troopers spent much of their first month in camp escorting supply trains, mail runs, and cattle herds.[6]

Construction of the new post was assigned to Capt. David W. Porter, assistant quartermaster for the Department of Texas, on December 10, 1867. Porter employed civilian masons and carpenters to construct temporary storehouses for quartermaster and commissary goods. Work began on the foundations for a permanent commissary in January 1868. While buildings remained under construction, the soldiers lived in tents or huts with their horses in temporary corrals. Open fireplaces heated many of the tents, although some troopers did manage to obtain heating stoves. The only permanent building in the spring of 1868 appears to have been the sutler's store, a general store run by a merchant under contract to provide some comforts to the soldiers. This structure, erected and opened for business as quickly as possible, had been "built of pickets, with green pecan board roof."[7]

At the request of Major Hatch, Huntt renamed the outpost Camp Kelly to honor Capt. Michael Kelly in January 1868. Kelly had died of typhoid fever on August 13, 1867, while commanding the first "Permanent Camp on the Rio Concho."[8] In March 1868 the construction site just north of Camp Kelly was officially designated Fort Concho by Secretary of War Edwin M. Stanton. Maj. George C. Cram replaced Huntt as commander of Fort Concho in March. Cram erected a temporary guardhouse of pecan wood and improved sanitation for the soldiers' quarters. His continued efforts to encourage construction of the permanent buildings met with little success. Captain Porter's responsibilities included construction at Forts Griffin and Richardson to the north, so he seldom remained at Fort Concho for an extended period. During his absences, Porter often left construction unsupervised. Without any direction, the civilian employees made little progress. Captain Huntt had already complained that "the expenses incurred at this Post for wages and rations of the men alone, amount to over fifty-six thousand dollars and the first stone not laid yet."[9]

Progress at the other posts under Porter's supervision proved just as slow. During 1868 more than 150 civilian masons and carpenters worked at Fort Richardson, yet the officers and men still lived in cottages of canvas-lined pickets. At Fort Griffin, about forty frame huts were built as temporary barracks. Many actually remained in use until the post was abandoned in 1881. Construction problems at the Texas outposts were complicated by the fact that supplies had to be freighted by oxen from Indianola on the Gulf Coast through San Antonio over rough and often

The first jail in San Angelo provides a good example of the use of wooden pickets in building. *Courtesy Fort Concho Library and Archives.*

muddy roads. Despite Major Cram's efforts to advance the building program at Fort Concho, little occurred during the summer of 1868. During this period Cram became involved in a feud with Ben Ficklin, the mail line superintendent, over Ficklin's use of government property and resources. When Cram placed Ficklin in the guardhouse, the postmaster general became involved. By August Major Cram had received a new assignment. Captain Porter also departed at about the same time, leaving construction of the three outposts barely begun.[10]

With Cram's reassignment, Maj. George A. Gordon, a former artillery officer, assumed command at Fort Concho. Gordon appointed Capt. Joseph Rendlebrock to take over the construction program. "Old Joe" Rendlebrock had served in the Prussian army before immigrating to the United States, where he enlisted in 1851 as a mounted rifleman. He rose through the ranks to become first sergeant in the Fourth Cavalry by the time of the Civil War. In 1862 he received a battlefield commission for meritorious service in Tennessee. By the end of the war Rendlebrock had risen to the rank of brevet major and was appointed regimental quartermaster for the Fourth Cavalry. His pre-war service on the frontier gave him the reputation "as an old and experienced Indian campaign-

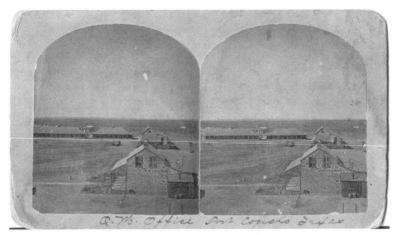

The quartermaster and commissary storehouses, the oldest structures at Fort Concho, can be seen in the upper right of this image. *Courtesy Fort Concho Library and Archives.*

er." "Old Joe" frequently assumed the task of instructing young officers during patrols, giving them pointers on frontier campaigning in his heavy German accent. At age forty-five, a veteran in all phases of army life, Rendlebrock proved an effective choice to take over the construction of Fort Concho.[11]

By the end of 1868 the quartermaster's storehouse, commissary, and one wing of the hospital building had been completed. The construction crews used native limestone quarried from an area south of the post. Mortar was made with lime extracted from the stone and crushed sandstone from along the Concho River. Most wood for framing still had to be shipped from the Gulf Coast. While sawmills along the Colorado River did produce some lumber locally, most of this was pecan wood, which proved difficult to use because of its hardness and the tendency of green wood to shrink and twist after it had been nailed in place.[12]

Captain Rendlebrock employed civilian stonemasons and carpenters to coordinate the construction efforts. Many of these were German immigrants from Fredericksburg, although the rolls also included a significant number of Scots and Irish. From 1869 to 1871 almost 90 percent of the civilian employees worked as craftsmen constructing the permanent buildings on post.[13] Between

OFFICERS' QUARTERS 3

Homes for the fort's officers were built in several stages with the last ones completed in the mid- to late-1870s. Officers' Quarters 3 may have been the first completed in March 1870. Until Officers' Quarters 1 was finished in 1872, this building served as the commanding officer's home. Rank definitely had its privileges as space in the way of rooms was assigned according to military rank, not family need. An unmarried major would get more space than a lieutenant with a large family. Because Officers' Quarters 3 has more original interior fabric than any other quarters on the row, museum staff chose to restore and furnish this structure with a period interior to show the life and times of an 1870s officer, his family, and a guest junior officer. During the annual Christmas event held the first weekend of December, the building is hosted by volunteers in period clothing with the soft glow of lanterns and lamps about them.

scouting expeditions and escort duties soldiers provided much of the unskilled labor. During 1869 troopers helped build five sets of officers' quarters and the first company barracks. In August Post Surgeon William Notson reported, "This month marks a new era—the actual occupation of quarters by the troops."[14]

In October 1869 work crews completed a frame building near the center of the parade ground designated as an office for the post adjutant and quartermaster. While the stone buildings rose slowly, many officers and enlisted men, following the example of other posts, built frame or picket structures to provide some solid shelter for their families. Noncommissioned officers, the baker, the drum major, and the chief musician all lived in frame buildings lined with canvas for insulation. Although most enlisted men remained single, some married soldiers did build homes, which in later years were described by a quartermaster as "temporary tumbledown buildings erected in most instances at the cost of their original occupants."[15]

Some of the officers moved into stone quarters in 1869. Families shared the available buildings, with captains and lieutenants authorized one room and a kitchen. A canvas or frame structure behind most of the stone quarters provided the kitchen. Single

This photograph shows three views: Fort Concho from a distance, Officers' Row, and Barracks Row. *Courtesy Fort Concho Library and Archives.*

officers were housed in the upper rooms of the hospital. During 1870 masons and soldiers built two more sets of officers' quarters and a second barracks. James Trainer, the post trader, built a large stone sutler's store west of the fort. Also completed in 1870 were a stone corral, stables, and a new guardhouse to replace the one made of pecan wood. Many officers had stone walls constructed to enclose the back yards of their homes. From the completed front porches on officers' row, the banks of the North Concho River could be seen past the wide parade ground and company barracks.[16]

In June 1870, while Maj. John Hatch commanded Fort Concho, he began to experiment with adobe as a possible substitute for limestone. Drying the brick in an open yard, he constructed walls around some of the quarters. A squad of troopers under the supervision of a commissioned officer could produce almost a thousand adobe bricks per day. This proved to be exhausting work, often more effort than quarrying limestone and making mortar. Hatch abandoned the use of adobe brick after "the heavy rains of August beat them to pieces, the freshets of the rivers

Wide view of Fort Concho during its active period. *Courtesy Fort Concho Library and Archives.*

washed away a good share, and the unsatisfactory material of which they were composed proved too fragile to enable them to be used for the purposes intended." His efforts earned him the nickname "Dobe" Hatch, however, which he carried throughout the remainder of his career.[17]

Major Hatch continued to push for the completion of post structures through the fall of 1870 on into 1871. A quartermaster's corral for mules and draft animals and a shed for the wagons were erected. Foundation work began for a blacksmith shop and other workshops. Permanent sinks to provide sanitary facilities for the enlisted men were constructed behind each barracks. Lumber arriving overland from San Antonio continued to present a problem. Surgeon Notson noted that while the lumber did arrive on schedule, "the wrong articles are invariably delivered . . . first delivered were shingles. The walls of four houses are as far forward as they can get until joist and rafters arrive, while sheathing and lathes are abundant."[18]

Notson's frustration with War Department bureaucracy increased in February 1872, when Fort Concho discharged most of its civilian masons and carpenters due to a reduction in funding. A force of more than sixty craftsmen dwindled to around fifteen, most of them carpenters, retained to complete structures already begun. Notson lamented the fact that "mechanics have been collected from far and wide in the country, at great trouble and

HEADQUARTERS BUILDING

For its first decade, Fort Concho lacked a formal administration building. The ambitious Colonel Grierson addressed that issue shortly after his arrival by having the headquarters constructed in 1876. It served as a nerve center for the post until abandonment in 1889. From 1878 to 1881 this building served as Headquarters for the District of the Pecos, an administrative region of vast territory that included Forts Davis, Stockton, and Griffin and eight sub-posts for the purpose of coordinating efforts to contain increased Indian activity along the frontier. After Fort Concho's closing the building served in many capacities, including as a rooming house in the early 1900s. When Mrs. Ginevra Wood Carson decided to move her West Texas Museum from the Tom Green County Courthouse in the late 1920s, she chose this building as its new home, beginning a nine-decade effort to acquire all of the original fort buildings and land. Today four of the rooms have been restored to their original appearance (court-martial room, orderly room, adjutant's office, and regimental head-quarters) while two other rooms have interpretive displays.

expense . . . and yet, as the season opens, they are discharged and scattered, for want of a small appropriation."[19]

Despite the loss of skilled labor, some construction did continue on the plateau where the rivers joined. By the end of 1872 Fort Concho consisted of barracks for eight companies, eight sets of officers' quarters, a hospital, guardhouse, powder magazine, bakery, storehouses, workshops, and stables. Company streets had been laid out and landscaping begun. Cedar, elm, pecan, and hackberry trees were planted and a post garden cultivated with moderate success.[20]

In April 1875 Fort Concho became headquarters for the Tenth Cavalry under Col. Benjamin Grierson. Grierson had previously undertaken a construction program at Fort Sill and would later complete the building of Fort Davis. At Fort Concho he began by thoroughly cleaning the parade ground and repairing the barracks. Workmen then moved the adjutant's office to the east end of the parade ground and erected a flagstaff in the center of the

Officers' row at Fort Concho. Captains' and lieutenants' families frequently shared the available houses. *Courtesy Fort Concho Library and Archives.*

field. In 1876 Grierson replaced the old wooden office with a stone administration building that included the regimental head-quarters, a court-martial room, and a post library for more than three hundred volumes "of a literary, historical and miscella-neous character."[21]

Grierson also ordered a forage house built and in 1877 added a double set of officers' quarters. In December 1878 workers com-pleted the last permanent building at Fort Concho on a foundation originally laid as the kitchen for a new set of officers' quarters. Chaplain George Dunbar described the new structure, designated a schoolhouse and chapel, as "by far the best finished room in the post." The commander also took a strong interest in gardening and landscaping. In 1879 he had a water pipe laid along officers' row and "a hydrant put on the parade ground so that water can be used fully and the grass kept green."[22]

Despite continuing efforts to improve the post, the completed buildings began to develop problems after several years of use. Windows in the barracks broke and in many cases were not repaired for several months. Plaster cracked and fell from the walls, which were then covered by "cotton cloth." With age, the hospital and some of the quarters became infested with bats. Work crews removed the bats and then sealed off cornices and spaces between the rafters with lumber to prevent them from returning.[23]

By May 1877, ten years after it was established, the outpost at the junction of the North and Middle Concho had cost the United States an estimated $1 million in construction costs. A correspondent for the *San Antonio Express* viewing Fort Concho at the height of its active period reported, "The post commands an extensive view of the country and at a distance it presents the appearance of a miniature city." The reporter continued describing "neat and commodious" quarters "constructed of gray stone of excellent quality."[24] Despite initial difficulties facing construction, Fort Concho finally rose above the West Texas landscape, ready to provide a vital link in the line of frontier defense.

2.
MACKENZIE'S RAIDERS: SECURING THE TEXAS FRONTIER

DURING THE EARLY YEARS at Fort Concho, construction duty proved to be a major focus in the troopers' daily routine. When not on construction crews or guard duty, the men of Fort Concho regularly scouted for Indians or acted as escorts for supply trains, mail runs, and cattle herds. Companies rotated field assignments at sites including old Fort Chadbourne, Johnson's Station, and Camp Charlotte, a stockaded outpost at the junction of the Butterfield and San Antonio–El Paso mail routes.[25]

Despite frequent scouting expeditions, troopers seldom actually encountered the Indian raiding parties that continued to attack stage routes and supply lines. In February 1871 Post Surgeon William Notson noted in his medical history that "some scouting was attempted with the usual negative results." Such discouraging accounts proved typical of army patrols from the Guadalupe Mountains to the Red River. Yet even as Notson wrote his entry, the Fourth Cavalry, under its new commander, Col. Ranald S. Mackenzie, had begun to develop a plan of retaliation against Comanche and Kiowa raiders. Following the Kiowa attack on the Warren wagon train in May 1871, the Fourth Cavalry joined in a coordinated campaign with troopers from Fort Griffin and Fort Sill. In July 1871 six troops, led by Company I commander Capt. Napoleon Bonaparte McLaughlin, marched to the Little Wichita River, where they joined the rest of the Fourth Cavalry in pursuit

Col. Ranald S. Mackenzie and the Fourth U.S. Cavalry mounted operations against the Comanches from Fort Concho in the early 1870s. *Courtesy the National Archives.*

of Indians who had left the Fort Sill reservation. Unfortunately, while serving as a good field exercise and lesson in geography, the expedition met with little success. The wagon train raiders had already returned to the reservation. McLaughlin's weary men turned back toward Fort Concho in September 1871.[26]

By the spring of 1872 Comanche and Kiowa raids had increased in what Colonel Mackenzie termed a "vigorous manner." Numerous scouting expeditions set out from Fort Concho, yet most returned to camp without seeing a single Indian. Then, on March 26, 1872, Sgt. William Wilson of Pennsylvania received orders to assemble a patrol that would follow the trail of some horses recently stolen near the post. Wilson's scout left Fort Concho the next day, picking up the horses' tracks about five miles from the fort. The month of March had been unusually warm and dry, and the trail remained easy to follow throughout the afternoon. Wilson established a dry camp for the night near the edge of the Colorado River valley.[27]

Wilson's patrol entered the valley early on the morning of March 28. They soon lost the trail, and Wilson decided to camp by the river for breakfast while their guide scouted ahead. As the patrol began to cook their meal, the guide suddenly rode back to report that Indians were camped on a nearby creek. In his report,

Wilson stated that he then "ordered to saddle up and started up a creek where I saw one man swimming, took up the gallop observing several men on the other side of the river which I crossed when we were fired into by a party of men. Returned the fire and ordered my men to charge."[28]

Wilson's men battled the party, which they believed to be hostile Indians, for almost half an hour. The troopers reported two of the enemy killed, three wounded, and one captured out of fourteen engaged in the skirmish. They also recaptured nineteen of the stolen horses and five mules. Upon questioning his prisoner, Wilson discovered that the party they had attacked were actually Comancheros, Hispanic or half-breed traders who bargained for stolen goods with the Indians. Herding the recaptured stock, the patrol traveled until late that night, camping five miles from the post. On March 29 they rode in, having covered 125 miles and completed one of the few successful scouting expeditions in recent months.[29]

Sergeant Wilson turned his prisoner over to the post commander, Major Hatch. Hatch soon realized how important this captive might be toward ending the increasing problem of Indian raiders. Under questioning, the prisoner identified himself as Apalonio Ortiz, a New Mexican, who was traveling with a group of traders from La Cuesta. He stated that they had crossed the western part of Texas by the Llano Estacado, considered by many in the army to be a barren desert. Upon reaching Muchaque, a high flat-topped hill in present-day Borden County, they found a Comanche and Mescalero encampment of more than one hundred lodges where Comancheros engaged in a regular business, trading guns, ammunition, and food for stolen cattle. Ortiz also confirmed that "there is plenty of water on the Staked plain, it is permanent, the road is a good one."[30]

Hatch proceeded to report this information to Colonel Mackenzie, the Military Department of Texas, and the District of New Mexico. At last the army had information on the location of Indian encampments and verification that the Staked Plains was not an uncrossable wasteland. In the hope of earning a pardon, Ortiz identified camps, springs, and waterholes all along the trail to New Mexico with approximate distances from one to the next. Hatch believed that by patrolling this trail, illegal trade with the Indians might be brought to a halt. In his letter to a friend in New York, he lamented the fact that the "virtuous citizens of New Mexico" trafficked freely in stolen cattle while the army chased blindly across the plains and commented, "How the savages must laugh when they talk among themselves of the want of common sense of the white race."[31]

To verify the Comanchero's story, Hatch sent Captain McLaughlin with two companies of the Fourth Cavalry and a detachment of the Eleventh Infantry to search for the Indian camp at Muchaque. On April 30, 1872, McLaughlin spotted three Indians from a distance. That same day Ortiz identified the trail to Muchaque, and the next day troopers found signs indicating the recent passage of a large herd of horses. Following the signs, they found horses in a nearby arroyo, guarded by Indians who fled at the sight of the soldiers. McLaughlin pursued the Indian guard for about two miles and found a large village that he estimated at 150 to 200 lodges—totally deserted. In the middle of the village troopers discovered a crude sign with "a strip of raw hide about two feet long, on the smooth side of which was rudely drawn a picture of a soldier" indicating that the Indians were aware of the soldiers' coming and were warning others of their band to stay away. McLaughlin's troops explored for several days, mapping the Colorado River and the edge of the Llano Estacado. They returned to Fort Concho on May 13.[32]

A week later, Major Hatch left the post to meet with Colonel Mackenzie and the Department of Texas commander, Gen. Christopher C. Augur, in San Antonio concerning recent developments. Following this "council of war," Augur issued orders on May 31, 1872. Mackenzie, with the Fourth Cavalry and elements of the Eleventh and Twenty-fourth Infantry, was to establish a supply camp in the field "with the view of breaking up the cattle stealing, and stopping the incursions of hostile Indians along the northern frontier of Texas." On June 17 Captain McLaughlin left Fort Concho with Companies D and I to rendezvous with Colonel Mackenzie on the Freshwater Fork of the Brazos River.[33]

Throughout June and July, McLaughlin scouted the headwaters of the Colorado River searching for fresh signs of the Comanches that had camped at Muchaque. Unfortunately, the frequent evening rains erased many recent trails. On July 28, 1872, five companies of the Fourth Cavalry embarked upon an expedition across the Llano Estacado. With Apalonio Ortiz as his guide, Colonel Mackenzie located a major cattle trail leaving Blanco Canyon and crossing the Staked Plains. Mackenzie later wrote, "It was not my intention to have come into this section of the country, but the trail was so plain that it appeared to me that it should be followed." His troops traced the route into New Mexico, where Mackenzie attempted to track down the Comancheros at Puerta de Luna without success. They returned by way of Tierra Blanca Creek to Palo Duro Canyon and through Quitaque. This proved to be the first United States exploration of the South Plains and eventually opened the area to Anglo settlement.[34]

By September 1872 Mackenzie had become certain that the Comanches were camped on the Red River, north of the area his troops had previously scouted. He left the headquarters camp with five companies of the Fourth Cavalry and one of the Eleventh Infantry on September 21. Proceeding past the Salt Fork of the Red River without incident, the column reached McClellan Creek on the North Fork on September 29. About two miles up the creek the troopers found fresh mule tracks, which they followed for almost twelve miles before sighting an Indian village around 4 P.M.[35]

Mackenzie ordered the command to attack at a gallop. Companies A, F, and L assaulted the center of the village, while Company D attempted to capture the Indians' horses. Company I formed on the right flank and attacked a smaller detached village. Sergeant Wilson and his troopers charged through the village, scattering the Comanches before them. Soldiers pursued the fleeing Indians until almost dark. Company F remained heavily engaged at the main encampment for more than half an hour until the Comanche warriors finally retreated, having been forced to leave many of their women and children behind. The Fourth Cavalry took 124 prisoners and captured most of the Indian horses.[36]

The battle at McClellan Creek was Colonel Mackenzie's first major victory over the Comanches. The night after the battle a few Indians managed to stampede and recapture most of their horses, robbing the Fourth Cavalry of some of the victors' spoils. The Indians regained their mobility and Mackenzie suffered an embarrassment that he would remember in coming campaigns. The Comanche women and children, however, remained the soldiers' prisoners. In his official report Colonel Mackenzie cited many of his officers and men for gallantry in action. Nine enlisted men, most of them from Companies F and I, received special commendation for distinguished conduct. One of those was Sgt. William Wilson, who had already received the Medal of Honor for his scouting action in March. When Mackenzie's report reached division commander Gen. Philip H. Sheridan, he recommended that all nine men receive Medals of Honor for their actions at McClellan Creek. On November 19, 1872, Sergeant Wilson received his second Medal of Honor, becoming the only soldier to ever receive the United States' highest military decoration twice in the same year.[37]

Companies D and I returned to Fort Concho on October 21 escorting 116 Indian women and children as prisoners. The quartermaster's stone corral, completed the previous year, provided a home for the captives through the winter of 1872–1873. Daily rations were provided and the army even approved some funds for clothing. Soldiers' families and local settlers visited the Indians, often bringing gifts of food, candy, or various trinkets. At the same time General Augur recommended that the prisoners be held "until all the white captives in the hands of any tribe south of the Arkansas be restored, and all public animals stolen during the past year be returned." Comanche warriors spent the winter trying to satisfy the government's demands, and for a while their raids all but ceased.[38]

By April 14, 1873, the Comanches had returned a sufficient number of captives and horses for the Department of Texas to order the release of prisoners from Fort Concho. Capt. Robert McClermont of the Eleventh Infantry commanded the escort for the Indian women and children. They left the post on May 24,

1873, for Fort Sill, Indian Territory, traveling through many Texas frontier settlements that had been victims of Comanche and Kiowa raids. Near Jacksboro, McClermont received word that angry settlers waited in town to prevent the prisoners from returning to their people. The veteran soldier entered Jacksboro and faced nearly a thousand irate citizens alone. While he pretended to await the arrival of his party, the wagons carrying Comanche women and children safely bypassed the town. They arrived at Fort Sill on June 10 for a joyous reunion with their families. The Comanche leaders thanked McClermont and praised him "for his care and kindness to them on the route."[39]

While McClermont reunited the Comanche families, Colonel Mackenzie had already embarked on another campaign with the Fourth Cavalry. In March 1873 he moved his command from Fort Concho to Fort Clark at present-day Brackettville near the Rio Grande. The Kickapoo Indians along the Rio Grande had conducted frequent raids north of the river and then returned to the safety of their villages on the Mexican side. In 1865 the Kickapoos had migrated south into Mexico. On January 8 of that year they defeated Texas militia at Dove Creek just west of the future site of Fort Concho. Once safely in Mexico, the Kickapoos were joined by Lipan Apaches and other displaced tribes in a succession of profitable raids on the Anglo settlements in Texas.[40]

By 1873 the raids had so seriously depleted Texas livestock along the border that General Sheridan insisted Mackenzie take whatever action proved necessary "to control and hold down the situation." Mackenzie immediately began drilling his troops for field duty while he sent scouts south of the border to locate the Indian villages. On the night of May 16, 1873, his scouts reported that a large party of warriors had left the Kickapoo and Lipan villages on the San Rodrigo River near El Remolino. Colonel Mackenzie assembled six companies of the Fourth Cavalry. He also called for aid from the Seminole-Negro Indian Scouts under Lt. John Bullis of the Twenty-fourth Infantry. The scouts had been recruited from a band of Seminoles and escaped slaves who settled near the Rio Grande in 1850. Mackenzie's command crossed into Mexico after dark the next day. They were soon forced to abandon their pack mules to maintain speed. Carrying only "hard bread," Mackenzie's raiders rode all night, arriving at the rim of the San Rodrigo valley just after daylight on May 18.[41]

Mackenzie quickly formed his command into platoons to attack the three Indian villages visible along the river. He assigned Capt. Napoleon B. McLaughlin and Company I from Fort Concho to lead the advance. McLaughlin, who fought with Mackenzie against the Comanches in 1872, had already proved himself a courageous and skillful commander. Dur-

Capt. Napoleon B. McLaughlin served with both the Fourth and Tenth Cavalry during their time at Fort Concho. *Courtesy Library of Congress.*

ing the Civil War he had served as brigadier general of volunteers and was cited for gallant and meritorious service at the battles of Chancellorsville and Gettysburg. Now he guided the Fourth Cavalry forward through patches of mesquite, yucca, and cactus toward the Kickapoo encampment at an ever increasing pace. Indian villagers quickly scattered before the charging troopers. The few warriors left to defend the lodges resisted briefly before falling to the soldiers. Company I pursued the escapees, while other companies collected the horses and burned the lodges in all three villages. When Mackenzie reassembled the command, he counted nineteen Indians dead, forty women and children prisoners, and sixty-five horses captured. Three of his soldiers suffered wounds, one of them severe.[42]

After resting for several hours, the Fourth Cavalry rode away from the smoldering villages. They followed a barren, unpopulated route to the Rio Grande in an attempt to avoid angry Mexican settlers or Indian warriors. They reached the river near dawn and began the slow process of crossing. Mackenzie's raiders had covered close to 160 miles in less than forty hours without food or sleep. General Sheridan strongly supported Mackenzie's actions south of the border. The Texas state legislature issued a resolution officially thanking him. The Mexican government did not retaliate or make any official protest. U.S. Indian commissioners resumed their negotiations with the Kickapoos and in July reached an agreement whereby part of the tribe was reunited with the women and children taken prisoner on a reservation in the United States. The Fourth Cavalry did not venture into Mexico again in force but continued to patrol the Rio Grande against raiding parties through early 1874.[43]

In July 1874 General Augur ordered the Fourth Cavalry back to Fort Concho to prepare for action against the Comanches, Kiowa, and Cheyenne in a campaign that became known as the Red River War. On June 27 more than two hundred Indians inspired by the Comanche medicine man Isatai had attacked buffalo hunters camped at the trading post of Adobe Walls in the Texas Panhandle. In an attempt to end the increasing number of raids on the South Plains, the army requested permission to pursue the Comanches and their allies onto reservation lands. The Secretary of War replied by ordering the punishment of all those considered renegades without regard to reservation boundaries. By August 1874 five columns consisting of more than three thousand soldiers had taken the field to converge on warriors camping in the Panhandle area.[44]

Col. Nelson Miles marched south from Fort Dodge with twelve companies; Maj. William Price led four companies of the Eighth Cavalry east along the Canadian River; Lt. Col. John Davidson moved west from Fort Sill with companies of the Tenth Cavalry and Eleventh Infantry; and Lt. Col. George Buell left Fort Griffin with eight companies moving northwest. The southern column under Colonel Mackenzie left Fort Concho on August 23. Eight companies of the Fourth Cavalry, four companies of the Tenth Infantry, and one of the Eleventh Infantry marched north across the plains to Mackenzie's old supply camp on the Freshwater Fork of the Brazos River. On September 19 they left the supply camp to follow trails located by the Seminole-Negro scouts. Throughout the next week, Mackenzie's troopers moved further north along the trail, hampered by frequent rains. On the night of September 26, 1874, Indians attacked the column camped at Tule Canyon. The colonel, aware of the presence of warriors in the area, had ordered the horses staked out to prevent a stampede while the men slept with their clothes on. The soldiers "very promptly met and repulsed" the attack, according to Mackenzie. Seeing that they could not panic the army's horses, the Indians withdrew but continued to fire on the camp from cover of darkness. Just after dawn they appeared on the hills around camp to resume the attack. Company E, accompanied by the scouts, mounted and charged, scattering the attackers. Under the command of Capt. Peter Boehm, who established the first permanent camp on the Concho in 1867, the troopers pursued for about three miles, killing one Indian and wounding several others.[45]

The next day the Fourth Cavalry continued to follow the attackers for several miles before going into camp. Mackenzie, convinced that the Indians were leading him away from their encampment, waited until after dark and then moved out to the northwest. Once again the soldiers rode all night. Before dawn scouts had found a clear trail leading to the edge of the canyons of the Red River. By daybreak Mackenzie's troopers reached the junction of Palo Duro and Blanca Cita canyons, where they looked down more than seven hundred feet at Comanche, Kiowa, and Cheyenne villages spread out along the canyon floor. Scouts located "a narrow, dizzy, winding trail," and the soldiers began a slow descent. Reaching the floor of Palo Duro Canyon, the first companies quickly mounted and charged into villages that were already being abandoned. They chased the fleeing Indians the length of the encampment, capturing their herd of more than fourteen hundred horses. Instead of continuing the pursuit, the colonel ordered all the lodges and supplies burned. After several years of hard campaign experience, Mackenzie had learned that the most effective way to defeat the Comanches was to destroy their resources so that they could not be reclaimed. His soldiers drove the Indian herd of horses out of the canyon to the plains, where 1,048 of them were slaughtered to prevent their recapture by the Comanches.[46]

The destruction of supplies and livestock at Palo Duro Canyon combined with successes by the columns under Colonel Miles and Colonel Buell effectively brought an end to the Comanche and Kiowa raids on the Texas plains. Mackenzie's column continued to patrol the Panhandle area until December 1874. The presence of five columns of soldiers prevented the Indians from restocking their supplies for the winter. Gradually they returned to the reservation and the soldiers returned to Fort Concho and other posts. By the beginning of 1875 Fort Concho had become a central link in the chain of army posts along the Texas frontier. Yet the Fourth Cavalry's essential role in developing the outpost on the Concho had come to an end. In early 1875 Mackenzie's regiment was reassigned to Fort Sill and the headquarters of the Tenth U.S. Cavalry came to Fort Concho.[47]

3.
SQUARELY FOUGHT: THE
DISTRICT OF THE PECOS AND
THE CAMPAIGN AGAINST
VICTORIO

COL. BENJAMIN GRIERSON ARRIVED at Fort Concho with the head-quarters of the Tenth Cavalry on April 17, 1875. Grierson, original-ly a music teacher from Illinois, had earned his reputation as a Union cavalry commander during the Civil War. In 1866 he orga-nized the Tenth Cavalry, one of two black mounted regiments in the Regular Army. In contrast to the Irish and German immigrants of the Fourth Cavalry, the Tenth consisted largely of former slaves from the border states of Virginia, Kentucky, Maryland, and Tennessee. To the army, the black troopers were known as Grierson's Brunets. Their Indian adversaries referred to them with respect as "buffalo soldiers" because their hair resembled that of the sacred buffalo.[48]

Since 1867 the Tenth Cavalry had been stationed in Kansas and Oklahoma. With the defeat of the Cheyennes and many of the Kiowas and Comanches during the Red River War, their area of operations moved south to the West Texas plains. At Fort Concho the Tenth assumed regular outpost and escort duties. Although the Comanches and Kiowas had been forced onto the reservation, Indian raids on local ranches and stage lines continued to pose a threat to expanding settlement in western Texas. Grierson's buffa-lo soldiers patrolled the South Plains and trans–Pecos regions

Col. Benjamin H. Grierson, commander of the Tenth U.S. Cavalry, directed the District of the Pecos from 1878–1881 at Fort Concho. *Courtesy Fort Concho Library and Archives.*

searching for raiding parties. While many of those expeditions were uneventful, one patrol in July 1877 actually proved disastrous for an entire company of troopers.

On July 4, 1877, Capt. Nicholas Nolan received orders to proceed with Company A to Big Spring and then on to the Llano Estacado in pursuit of "bands of marauding Indians found in that section." Nolan established a supply camp on Bull Creek northeast of Muchaque with twenty troopers. The remainder of his company scouted the plains for signs of the elusive warriors. On July 26, while at Double Lakes, Nolan received word from buffalo hunters that the Indians had been sighted traveling northeast. Although the summer had been particularly dry, Nolan apparently did nothing to insure that his soldiers filled their canteens or carried extra water. Instead, they set out in the heat of the afternoon, following the trail of about forty Indians. By the next evening, after thirty hours without fresh water, many of the command were suffering from heat exhaustion. The trail they followed had split into many "ill-defined tracks." Nolan sent his guide, José Tafoya, ahead to find water and made camp for the night.[49]

When Tafoya had not returned by morning, Nolan decided to turn back toward Double Lakes for water. As Dr. Joseph King later reported, the men had become so desperate that "the most loathsome fluid would now have been accepted to moisten their swollen tongues and supply their inward craving." Some began to drink their own urine or even the horses' urine sweetened with sugar. As some of the horses began to struggle and die, the troopers cut them open and drank their thickening blood. Confused and suffering, Nolan's command staggered on through the parched heat of the open plains. Finally, around 5 A.M. on July 30, the first members of the straggling column reached Double Lakes. They had been without water for eighty-six hours. Captain Nolan sent men back with canteens of water to bring in the rest of his command. Some of the scattered soldiers failed to reach Nolan's supply camp until several days later. When all had been recovered, the total loss was four troopers, twenty-three horses, and four mules. The disastrous expedition had cost the Tenth Cavalry more lives than most Indian engagements.[50]

Yet even as Nolan's men recovered from their nightmare journey, scouting parties from Fort Concho had already begun to shift their focus from the Staked Plains to the developing trans–Pecos region. Apaches from the Mescalero and San Carlos reservations had long considered it natural during food shortages to leave the reservation on hunting or even raiding parties and then return as they pleased. In the mid-1870s they conducted an increasing number of raids across Texas from the Guadalupe Mountains to the Rio Grande. By January 1878 the situation had become serious enough that the army created the District of the Pecos to control what they considered the Apache problem and to promote settlement in western Texas. Colonel Grierson became commander of the new district with headquarters at Fort Concho.[51]

To deal with the Apaches, Grierson established a series of subposts at strategic locations throughout the District of the Pecos. In March 1878 he dispatched Company H under Capt. Louis H. Carpenter from Fort Davis to locate a site for a permanent post "at some point on the Eastern slope of the Guadalupe Mountains." Carpenter, who was familiar with the area from previous scouts, chose Bull Springs near the old Pine Springs overland mail station. On September 12 Capt. Thomas C. Lebo moved the permanent camp to Pine Springs in sight of the stage station ruins. Lebo stated

OFFICERS' QUARTERS 1

Officers' Quarters 1, constructed in 1872, replaced Officers' Quarters 3 as the commanding officer's home. Located at the southwest corner of the post, the two-story structure offered its occupant a far-reaching vista of his command. Col. Benjamin H. Grierson lived there longest as he commanded the post from 1875 to 1882. During his term the west office was added to the building, a kitchen and carriage house were built, and locks were installed on the doors. The Grierson family suffered a tragedy at the post on September 9, 1878, when their daughter Edith died in an upstairs bedroom after battling typhoid fever. When the fort was abandoned in 1889 Officers' Quarters 1 fell into civilian hands. The Fort Concho Museum purchased the property in 1964, and the Tom Green County Historical Society met in the building for many years. In 1994 the structure was fully renovated and restored as the Concho Valley Pioneer Heritage Center, open for special events and programs while serving as VIP quarters for Fort Concho and city of San Angelo guests.

that there was "an abundant supply of water . . . sufficient for supplying four or five companies of cavalry" and the grazing was "very fine indeed."[52]

While Lebo developed the Pine Springs outpost, troops also manned stations at Eagle Springs, Seven Springs, Peña Colorado, and Grierson's Spring. Grierson's Spring, located between the Concho and Pecos rivers, had been discovered by two ranchers pursuing cattle thieves earlier that year. Grierson sent out patrols to verify the spring's existence and in July 1878 ordered Capt. William B. Kennedy with Company F to occupy the site as a subpost. Dr. Samuel Smith described the spring as being at the head of a rock canyon where "the rock appears everywhere and crops out in the sides of the canyon, and has fallen down and blocked up what probably was in Noah's time, a stream." Yet the location proved to be of strategic value and by 1879 several stone buildings stood at Grierson's Spring.[53]

The subposts assumed even more importance when Ojo Caliente and Mescalero Apaches under Victorio left the San Carlos reservation to find refuge in the Guadalupe Mountains. Since 1877

The parade ground and bandstand at Fort Concho. The parade ground was the site for drills and formations by the troops throughout each day. *Courtesy Fort Concho Library and Archives.*

the Ninth Cavalry in New Mexico had attempted to contain Victorio's elusive Apaches. By the fall of 1879 the roving band had an established route across the trans–Pecos region between the Sacramento Mountains and Mexico. Colonel Grierson received word in October that "a large party of Indians were moving southward along the Rio Grande" with the intent of reaching the Mescalero reservation by way of Eagle Springs southeast of present-day Sierra Blanca. He immediately sent Captain Carpenter to establish his field quarters at the Eagle Springs subpost "with orders to attack and destroy, or vigorously pursue any Indians who might make their appearance in that section of the state." At the same time, Grierson recommended that the force in the Guadalupe Mountains "should be considerably increased."[54]

As Colonel Grierson positioned his troops for action, the Apaches continued to attack ranches and stage lines throughout the trans–Pecos. Victorio's situation in 1880 appears to have been a prime example of government mismanagement in Indian affairs. As leader of the Ojo Caliente or Warm Springs Apaches, Victorio had agreed to live on a reservation in his homeland of western New Mexico. In 1877, however, a move toward the consolidation of Indian lands

Victorio, chief of the Warm Springs Apaches, whose poor treatment on the reservations caused him to lead a band of renegade Apaches on raids across western Texas and New Mexico in 1879–1880. *Courtesy the National Archives.*

forced the Warm Springs band onto the San Carlos reservation in Arizona. Conditions there proved intolerable, and Victorio soon escaped, taking most of his people with him. They settled on the Mescalero reservation briefly in 1879, but when Victorio learned that he might be arrested for horse stealing and murder, he escaped once again with more than one hundred warriors and their families. By 1880 he had become a determined and experienced leader.[55]

On March 23, 1880, Colonel Grierson left Fort Concho with five companies of the Tenth Cavalry and a detachment of the Twenty-fifth Infantry. The troopers' objective was the Fort Stanton reservation, where they were to assist in disarming and dismounting Mescaleros believed to be providing Victorio with supplies. Grierson's column passed through Pecos Falls, Texas, on March 31, where they learned that Indians had stolen stock from nearby ranches only the night before. Grierson dispatched Lt. Calvin Esterly with a patrol to follow the Apache raiders. On April 3, 1880, in the middle of a severe dust storm, Esterly attacked the raiding party and recovered eight head of stock. He rejoined the main column on April 6 near the mouth of the Black River. That day, Company K under Captain Lebo set out to scout along the line of march, covering "a belt of country over fifty miles wide." Lebo found extensive signs of Apache raiding parties. He followed one recent trail into the Guadalupe Mountains and on April 9 overtook the Indians at Shake-Hand Springs. During the resulting fight, Company K destroyed the Apache camp. They killed the party's leader, captured four women and one child, and recovered a Mexican captive.[56]

Grierson's main column arrived in the vicinity of the Mescalero reservation on April 12, 1880. Heavy storms over the next two days delayed the disarming of Victorio's supporters until the afternoon of April 16. Grierson was ordered to stand ready. Three shots would be fired as a signal in case of trouble. Grierson received the signal that the Mescaleros were attempting to escape around 2:30 P.M. The Tenth Cavalry immediately moved forward across the Tularosa River and attacked the Mescaleros as they fled into the surrounding mountains. The attempt to disarm the Apaches before they could join Victorio had failed. Although Grierson's troopers captured and disarmed more than 250 Indian men, women, and children, many eluded the soldiers. Detachments of the Ninth and Tenth Cavalry pursued the Apaches into the mountains. Lt. Mason M. Maxon overtook one group and drove them back toward the reservation, killing one warrior and capturing five horses. Grierson remained in southern New Mexico until April 27, 1880, when the Tenth Cavalry returned to Texas. Captain Kennedy and Company F were left to man the outpost in the Guadalupe Mountains.[57]

On May 16 Grierson returned to his headquarters at Fort Concho. He instructed Company M at the head of the North Concho to "keep out detachments in all directions . . . to give any marauders a warm reception in case they should make their appearance in your section of the country." In June nineteen Pueblo Indians recruited as scouts at the Isleta mission near El Paso also took the field under the command of Lt. Frank H. Mills of the Twenty-fourth Infantry. While en route to Fort Davis they were attacked by about twenty Apaches at Viejo Pass. Hidden by rocks, the Indians killed one scout and three horses before retreating. Mills could not pursue them, as some of his scouts still had not been issued arms.[58]

Meanwhile, Col. Edward Hatch of the Ninth Cavalry, his troops exhausted by fruitless patrols, requested that the Tenth return to New Mexico. Grierson protested and managed to convince General Sheridan that his soldiers would be more effective against Victorio in western Texas. Colonel Grierson's plan was to patrol all the springs and waterholes in the trans–Pecos region in an attempt to keep the Apaches from water and force them back into Mexico. Troopers also reoccupied abandoned Fort Quitman on the Rio Grande as a temporary outpost. On June 17, 1880, a battalion of the Tenth Cavalry led by Captain Nolan arrived at Fort Concho from temporary duty at Fort Sill. Grierson described Nolan's command as "not more than half mounted, poorly armed and equipped, and entirely without pack mules." Despite their condition, the colonel needed Nolan's battalion in the field to keep Victorio from water. He managed to resupply them immediately and by June 27 issued orders for the command to proceed to the Guadalupe Mountains on patrol.[59]

On July 10, 1880, Colonel Grierson left Fort Concho with an escort that included his teenage son Robert and his adjutant, Lt. William H. Beck. They reached Fort Davis a week later and Eagle Springs on July 23. While there, the colonel communicated with Mexican Col. Adolfo Valle and agreed to intercept any Apaches crossing into Texas. On July 27 Grierson's party arrived at Fort Quitman. The next morning they were shocked to find Colonel Valle's forces on the opposite bank of the Rio Grande, weary and without provisions. Grierson instructed his quartermaster to issue the Mexican troops 1,000 pounds of flour, 500 pounds of oats, and 630 pounds of corn.[60]

With Colonel Valle no longer in pursuit of the Apaches, Grierson believed that Victorio would cross the river and head north. On July 29, 1880, with an escort of seven men and his son Robert, Grierson set out for Eagle Springs. Near Devil's Ridge at Tinaja de las Palmas, also known as Eighteen Mile Waterhole, they sighted a single Indian. Grierson established camp, believing that Victorio might be moving in that direction. After sending for reinforcements, the small party of soldiers fortified a ridge overlooking the watering place. On a strategic spot, called "Rocky Point" by Robert Grierson, the troopers built two stone breastworks and named them Forts "Beck" and "Grierson."[61]

Around 4 A.M. on July 30 Lt. Leighton Finley and a detachment of fifteen soldiers arrived to escort Colonel Grierson's party to safety. Instead of leaving, however, the colonel had Finley build a fortified position lower on the ridge and sent two of his men to speed reinforcements from Eagle Springs. A force of sixty Apaches appeared around 9 A.M. Seeing the cavalry positioned in the rocks, they attempted to cross the nearby stage road and move away from the waterhole. Grierson sent Finley with ten men to draw the Indians into a fight until reinforcements could arrive. Capt. Charles Viele and Company C reached the scene about an hour later. His advance party mistook Finley's troops for Indians and fired at them, forcing them back to the rock fortifications. Soon realizing their mistake, Viele's company engaged the Apaches and kept them from moving northward until Captain Nolan's company arrived. With troops attacking them from both sides, Victorio's band retreated and recrossed into Mexico. Grierson's scouts followed as far as the Rio Grande.[62]

Expecting the Apaches to make another thrust toward the Guadalupes, Grierson consolidated his forces at Eagle Springs. On August 2 Captain Carpenter sent a patrol under Cpl. Asa Weaver toward the Rio Grande to locate the Apaches. Near dawn the following day Weaver discovered Victorio's men near Alamo Spring. A fifteen-mile running battle ensued. Every few miles Weaver would take a new position and turn and fire on the Indians, checking their progress, and then charge on to the next position. By the time his patrol reached camp every horse had been hit and one trooper was wounded in the foot. Pvt. Willie Tockes died fighting when his injured horse turned and stampeded right into the Apache warriors. Based on Weaver's information, Colonel Grierson decided to march his main column to the Van Horn Mountains where they could intercept Victorio. Shortly after midnight on the morning of August 5, 1880, the column received word that the Apaches had slipped past them to the west. Knowing that Victorio would head for the nearest permanent watering place, Grierson mounted his men at 3 A.M. and made a sixty-five-mile forced march to the north. "Covered by a curtain of hills," they arrived at Rattlesnake Springs near the mouth of a canyon in the Sierra Diablo less than twenty-one hours later.[63]

After a brief rest and some food, Captain Viele, commanding Companies C and G, proceeded down Rattlesnake Canyon to intercept the Apaches, who were still unaware that they had been outflanked. Viele positioned his men at a high point in the canyon guarding the approaches to the spring. Around 2 P.M., close to sixty Indians appeared, advancing cautiously. The cavalry opened fire. After some initial confusion, the Apaches realized that only two small companies opposed them and attacked in force. Before the soldiers could be pushed back, Captain Carpenter moved the rest of the battalion into place. Company H dispersed among the rocks while Company B charged the Apaches, driving them back into the surrounding hills and ravines. At that point, Carpenter estimated almost one hundred Indian warriors and ninety troopers on opposite sides of the canyon. Around 4 P.M. Colonel Grierson's supply train appeared from the far side of the hills east of the Sierra Diablo. A dozen Apaches broke out of concealment to attack the train, but soldiers forced them back into the rocks. Carpenter then dismounted all of his troops and advanced in line of battle on the Indian positions. Reaching the rocks, the soldiers discovered that most of Victorio's force had retreated down the canyon. Horses were brought up as quickly as possible, but the Apaches had disappeared into the hills.[64]

The next day Grierson sent Carpenter and three companies of the Tenth to Sulphur Springs to prevent the Indians from continuing their move north. Shortly thereafter Captain Lebo arrived at Rattlesnake Springs, having captured Victorio's supply camp in the Sierra Diablo on August 3, 1880. Following his route, Captain Carpenter found a recent trail leading southwest on August 11. By that point both men and horses were exhausted. Sgt. John Casey later recounted, "While travelling over an unknown trail over sage brush, sand and alkali, we became very thirsty and very nearly perished from lack of water, as we had no fresh water, nothing but salty water for two days."[65] Rain that evening refreshed the weary troopers, yet they could not reach the Rio

Grande until August 13. Victorio's band had crossed the river the night before. Grierson wanted to follow the Indians into Mexico and defeat them while they remained in a weakened state. Diplomatic considerations, however, did not allow for such a move. The Tenth Cavalry remained in the field through the end of 1880 but did not encounter Victorio again. On October 18 Col. Joaquim Terrazas, commanding Chihuahua State Troops, telegraphed that he had attacked the Apache band in the Castillo Mountains four days before, "leaving Victorio, 60 warriors and 18 women and children dead."[66]

Although he had not taken part in the final defeat of Victorio, Grierson's decisive victories at Tinaja de las Palmas and Rattlesnake Springs played a major role in removing the Apache threat to Texas settlements. Nearly five hundred soldiers from the District of the Pecos had marched more than ten thousand miles protecting the springs and waterholes from Victorio's raiders in the last Indian campaign conducted on Texas soil. By the end of 1880 Grierson's command had also built and maintained more than a thousand miles of road and two hundred miles of telegraph lines across the trans–Pecos region. On February 7, 1881, the District of the Pecos was officially disbanded. Colonel Grierson relinquished his command stating, "A settled feeling of security, heretofore unknown, prevails throughout Western Texas." In only a few years the frontier had moved west, leaving Fort Concho in the midst of a rapidly developing area. In July 1882 the buffalo soldiers of the Tenth Cavalry followed, moving their headquarters further west to Fort Davis.[67]

4.
FORT CONCHO BLUES: THE
SOLDIERS' LIFE ON POST

THROUGH ALL THE SCOUTING EXPEDITIONS, explorations, and Indian campaigns, the daily routine of army life continued at Fort Concho. Soldiers woke to the sounds of a "morning gun" and the bugles blowing reveille at sunrise. After breakfast, the garrison assembled to post the guard. Officers inspected the companies and their quarters. Those soldiers not on guard performed various fatigue duties including the cleaning and repair of equipment and buildings, hauling wood and supplies, and care of the animals. The largest meal of the day was served around noon. Soldiers then returned to fatigue and guard duties for several hours followed by military drills and target practice until sunset. At dusk retreat sounded and supper was served. In the summer the day ended around 8:30 P.M. During the winter, with limited daylight, the soldiers' day ended even earlier.[68]

At all of the posts along the frontier this general routine was followed. To sustain them in their duties, the troopers received a daily ration that consisted mainly of beef, bread, and coffee. Even at breakfast, beef and bread remained the standard fare. For supper, soldiers ate food warmed over from the large noon meal. When possible, cooks supplemented the unappetizing ration with potatoes, bacon, hominy, bean soup, and even fresh fruits and vegetables. Gardens were cultivated on the post with some success, while officers pooled company funds to provide occasional delicacies. Soldiers returning from hunting trips sometimes brought fresh game, including buffalo, antelope, and turkey.[69] Yet

The family of Lt. Charles L. Cooper, Tenth U.S. Cavalry, who served at Fort Concho. His daughter, Forrestine "Birdie" Cooper, wrote her memoirs of life on post. *Courtesy Fort Concho Library and Archives.*

BARRACKS ROW

Within the first few years of Fort Concho's establishment, soldiers and professional craftsmen built six sets of barracks for the enlisted men. The first two built were cavalry barracks with double bays split by a central entrance featuring a "sally port" through which the troops could lead their mounts to the stables in the rear. The last four were single-room infantry barracks. Today the two cavalry barracks serve as the Visitor Center and special display space. The two remaining infantry barracks include a fully restored soldiers' home of the 1870s, complete with a period mess hall. The middle two barracks have been missing for nearly a century, although the fort's master plan does call for their reconstruction.

the supply of vegetables and items such as butter, honey, or lemons remained scarce.

In 1879 Surgeon Samuel Smith commented that he was "boarding at a first class dyspeptic factory," referring to the numerous cases of indigestion among soldiers at Fort Concho. While the bread generally received satisfactory or even complimentary reports from post surgeons, beef was "indifferent" at best. In 1877 Surgeon Joseph King complained, "The Fresh Beef now being issued is old, tough and too lean." Samuel Smith attributed some of the dietary problems to food preparation, lamenting, "Grease predominates and the spatter of the frying pan can be heard uttering its dulcet tones every morning, noon & night."[70]

Despite the dull routine and inadequate food, troopers at Fort Concho found ways to survive the monotony of life on a frontier outpost. Drinking and gambling proved to be common activities. Between pay periods, when money was scarce, gamblers would play for tobacco, cartridges, or even clothing. More civilized attempts to provide a social life on post included dances, theatricals, and holiday festivities. The Fourth of July, which was a favorite occasion at military posts across the nation, was often celebrated with horse races, foot races, and picnics. The Sixteenth Infantry band even provided entertainment for the first community Independence Day celebration in San Angelo.[71] On post, companies would take turns hosting dances or dinners. Music provided an important diversion, even when the only accompaniment available was a guitar or banjo played around the campfire. At various times during their periods of service, the Fourth and Tenth Cavalry and the Sixteenth Infantry each had a regimental band stationed at Fort Concho. Bands played when the troops entered the post or left, during formal parades, or just to entertain the garrison. Cavalry troops performed many of their duties to such popular tunes as "The Girl I Left Behind Me" and "The Regular Army, Oh!"[72]

Patrick F. Conway, born in County Clare, Ireland, January 17, 1852, enlisted in the Eighth U.S. Cavalry in 1883. Conway liked the West, particularly the growing town of San Angelo, and made it his home until his death in 1946. *Courtesy Fort Concho Library and Archives.*

Army officers' wives, seeking relief from the rugged, solitary existence on post, hosted many of the social activities, including receptions, dances, and holiday feasts. Many of the officers stationed at Fort Concho brought their wives and families to share life on the frontier. This led to frequent overcrowding in the officers' quarters. Forrestine "Birdie" Cooper, daughter of Lt. Charles L. Cooper, a junior officer on post, remembered that because of rank, their family with three children occupied the "short side" of one set of quarters consisting of a large living room, a small dining area, a tent for the kitchen, and one large bedroom upstairs. Despite the sometimes adverse conditions, officers' children at Fort Concho remained a common sight, working and playing without "the necessity of acknowledging bugle calls from sunrise to taps."[73] Families were less common among the enlisted men. Army regulations prevented married men from enlisting; however, veteran soldiers did marry with the permission of their commanding officer. Many of the enlisted men's wives worked on the post as married

Sergeant Fletcher of Company C, Sixteenth U.S. Infantry, while stationed at Fort Concho. *Courtesy Fort Concho Library and Archives.*

officers' servants or laundresses. Employing non-commissioned officers' wives as company laundresses became so widespread throughout Texas that in 1876 Gen. Edward O. C. Ord declared many of his best soldiers would be unable to reenlist if their wives were not also provided work.[74]

One occasion anticipated with great enthusiasm by all of the soldiers and their families was the arrival of the army paymaster. By regulation, the garrison was paid once every two months. While conditions on the frontier sometimes delayed the paymaster for several months, Fort Concho appears to have been visited on a fairly regular schedule. Even sub-posts and scouting expeditions could look forward to regular paydays. Samuel Smith reported the presence of the paymaster at Grierson's Spring in 1879 accompanied by an escort "armed with double barreled breach loading shot guns, a new weapon for the army, but very effective against the approach of stage robbers."[75]

Regular troop rotations between the army outposts brought companies from five regiments of cavalry and ten infantry regiments to Fort Concho. At various times the post was headquarters for the Fourth and Tenth Cavalry and the Eleventh and Sixteenth Infantry. A glance at the 1870 census shows the composition of those companies present for duty. In the Fourth Cavalry more than two thirds of the enlisted men were between the ages of twenty-one and thirty. Half of the troopers listed foreign countries as their birthplace, with almost half of those being Irish. Others came from Prussia and the German states, England, Canada, France, Wales, and Sweden. In the Eleventh Infantry soldiers were similar in age but fewer were foreign born. Many of the infantrymen came from New York, Ohio, Pennsylvania, and other states that had provided the Union with large numbers of volunteers during the Civil War.[76]

All four black regiments in the regular army served at Fort Concho. The 1880 census lists three fourths of the troopers in the Tenth Cavalry between the ages of twenty-one and thirty. One third of these claimed to be mulatto or of mixed parentage rather than black. Many registered their occupation prior to enlistment as laborer, while others had worked as farmers, shoemakers, barbers, blacksmiths, and waiters. Most came from the border states, especially

Born a slave in 1849, Sancho Mazique served as a carpenter in the Tenth U.S. Cavalry at Fort Concho 1875–1880. He later settled in San Angelo, where he died at the age of 101 in 1951. *Courtesy Fort Concho Library and Archives.*

Virginia, Kentucky, Maryland, and Tennessee. Those from the South predominantly came from Georgia.[77] White officers throughout the army had mixed feelings about the black soldiers who served under them. Surgeon William Notson observed that in drill the black troops were "decidedly superior" and that they excelled at all forms of music, "though sometimes sacrificing the military exactness to sweetness of execution." Yet he despaired that most would not make "intelligent soldiers" and commented that "the discipline and police of the post is too poor to decently condemn." Notson did notice a marked improvement in discipline and performance after the arrival of Lt. Col. William R. Shafter of the Twenty-fourth Infantry, an officer experienced in the command of black troops.[78]

William Veck's general store provided entertainment and supplies for the soldiers and brought settlers to the site that would later become San Angelo. *Courtesy Fort Concho Library and Archives.*

In 1880 Capt. William George Wedemeyer of the Sixteenth Infantry commented that although many soldiers of the black Tenth Cavalry appeared to be "natural thieves," they "are fairly well set up, drilled and disciplined and our men get along with them much better than I expected." Though few problems arose between black and white enlisted men of these veteran regiments, Wedemeyer did note that some of the Tenth's white officers openly treated their own men with contempt.[79] Such deplorable behavior from some officers did little to inspire the troopers of the Tenth. Still, the army provided better opportunities for African American men of the period than most occupations. Through their military service, many black recruits gained education, experience, and some measure of respect.

While many recruits did attempt to improve their situation, thieves, gamblers, and other "human sharks" frequently preyed upon soldiers with drinking or gambling habits and money in their pockets. Sometimes such habits led to time in the guardhouse. Court-martial records for the Fourth Cavalry in 1871 recall Pvt. Thomas Reger, who had spent 326 of his 401 days on duty in confinement for intoxication. In 1883 prisoner Tracy Williams faced court-martial with the notation, "So drunk had to be carried back to guard house." During 1882 and 1883 court-martial offenses at Fort Concho included six cases of intoxication, six thefts, one case of sleeping on guard, and five cases of assault. One of the assault charges was against Michael Hackett of the Sixteenth Infantry band, who "did unlawfully, maliciously and with violence assault, beat, bruise and wound Pvt August Miller." Hackett received six months confinement at hard labor for this offense. Other common sentences included forfeiture of pay, confinement in the guardhouse, or even dishonorable discharge from the service.[80]

Deserters almost always faced a dishonorable discharge and imprisonment. Despite the certainty of punishment, desertion continued to be a problem at all of

A lonely soldier stands beside the Concho River near Fort Concho. *Courtesy Fort Concho Library and Archives.*

the posts on the harsh, isolated Texas frontier. In July 1871 Surgeon William Notson reported twenty-three cases of desertion from Fort Concho. Although that proved to be an unusually high number, court-martial reports list desertion as one of the most frequent offenses throughout the post's active period. Black soldiers tended to desert less often, perhaps because they saw the army as a way to improve their condition. From July 1 to September 30, 1884, the Department of Texas reported sixty-five desertions. During the same period at Fort Concho, six soldiers deserted from the four companies of the Sixteenth Infantry while not one deserted in the two companies of the black Tenth Cavalry.[81]

The isolated conditions that caused many to desert gradually disappeared as nearby settlements grew up at Benficklin, Lone Wolf, and Veck's store. As early as February 1870 Doctor Notson reported the attempt by Bartholomew J. DeWitt, a government contractor, to establish a town just across the North Concho River from the post. The village, known as Saint Angela for DeWitt's wife or simply "Over the River," appeared to be almost completely made up of former post sutlers opening new stores and saloons to attract the soldiers' business. Such establishments also attracted many of the less desirable citizens on the Texas frontier. Birdie Cooper described William Veck's store as a place where "frontier characters came to buy tobacco, ammunition and arms—but principally to get whiskey and to gamble where there was no law to restrain them."[82]

Cooper also remembered men riding along the river firing their weapons in the direction of the post and crying insults to the soldiers. By the end of 1871 Notson claimed that more than one hundred murders had been committed "within a radius of ten miles from the Adjutant's office" during his tenure at Fort Concho, the most recent when "a man called another a louse." In 1878, even though the town now known as San Angela had begun to prosper, conditions remained so violent that Samuel Smith stated, "It is never considered safe to pass through there at night and no officer ever thinks of leaving the garrison after dark."[83]

With the enlisted men spending much of their off duty time in San Angela, inevitably soldiers became the victims of gamblers, ruffians, and even murderers. The incidents, which occurred in January and February 1881, reflect the continuing friction between the town and the army. Problems began with the murder of Pvt. Hiram Pinder, a member of Captain Wedemeyer's company, on January 19, 1881. Pinder was shot when he tried to stop Pleas Watson, a traveling gambler, from striking a black trooper of the Tenth. Although Watson was quickly captured, the situation had no time to cool down before a second murder was committed on January 31.[84]

Pvt. William Watkins of the Tenth Cavalry frequently played the banjo, danced, and sang in San Angela to earn extra money. On the night of January 31, 1881, he entertained a local sheep rancher, Tom McCarthy, and some of his friends. All of the men were drinking, and Watkins may have provoked McCarthy by attempting to grab his pistol. In any case, McCarthy shot him in the head. Watkins died instantly. McCarthy, still in shock, fled across the river, where he was arrested by the guard at Fort Concho. After an autopsy showed that his pistol had killed Watkins, he was turned over to Sheriff James Spears in San Angela.[85]

Established by Ernest Nimitz in 1878, the Nimitz Hotel became a hot spot during the Soldiers' Riot of 1881, when troopers searching for Tom McCarthy fired nearly two hundred shots into the building. *Courtesy Fort Concho Library and Archives.*

On February 2 the men of Fort Concho buried William Watkins. That night Wedemeyer's company, many with "blacked faces," and around a hundred soldiers from other companies marched into town. They captured Sheriff Spears and demanded McCarthy, but the sheriff had successfully hidden him. The soldiers returned to post without further incident, passing a patrol sent to bring them back. The next day a preliminary hearing began. Afraid that some of McCarthy's friends would try to release him, the soldiers made sure that they were seen in force along the river during their mounted drills. On the evening of February 4, 1881, Capt. Thomas Rose and his company escorted the sheriff and his prisoner to the jail at Benficklin. Just as the situation seemed under control, rumors began to circulate that McCarthy had been released and was at the Nimitz Hotel in town. Shortly before taps, thirty to forty troopers took weapons from the arms rack and crossed the river in the darkness. By the time the post could be alerted, they had fired "about 200 shots" into the Nimitz Hotel and surrounding buildings.[86]

Again, most of the soldiers returned to the post before military patrols could find them. An inquiry did identify five leaders of the attack on San Angela and they were placed in confinement. On February 5 Texas Rangers arrived to assist in maintaining order and an uneasy truce settled over the town and the post. As post commander, Colonel Grierson was admonished for not reporting the incident fully to his superiors and was warned that the army would not tolerate any continuation of violence against civilians. Grierson did cooperate with civil authorities to investigate the soldiers' attack, but no indictments were returned. By November, when a jury in Junction, Texas, found Tom McCarthy "not guilty," the post and town had developed some degree of cooperation. Yet, even as late as 1886, Captain Wedemeyer reported that a soldier "had his throat cut and was killed at the White Elephant Saloon in San Angelo."[87]

As the settlement of Saint Angela grew, it went through several name changes. By 1880 it was commonly known as San Angela. When the town applied for a post office as San Angela in 1881, postal officials refused to approve a name that did not follow the rules of Spanish grammar and the town became San Angelo. As San Angelo grew, the daily routine of army life continued at Fort Concho. Across the river, citizens of the new county seat could hear the steady beat of drums and blast of bugles from dawn to dark each day, calling the soldiers to their daily tasks in defense of the fading frontier.

5.
CIVILIZING THE FRONTIER: CHAPLAINS, SURGEONS, AND SUTLERS

ON APRIL 30, 1871, THREE WEEKS after his arrival at Fort Concho, Chaplain Norman Badger ventured across the North Concho River to conduct worship services in the small collection of saloons and shanties that later would become the city of San Angelo. Post Surgeon William Notson noted in his monthly report that it was "probably the first time that the name of the Deity was ever publicly used in reverence in that place."[88] Although not in the front line of battle or even in the post chain of command, the chaplains and others such as surgeons and sutlers who served at Fort Concho struggled to develop an atmosphere of civilization on the edge of the Texas frontier.

Since the army had funding for no more than about thirty post chaplains, they were assigned only to the most remote locations. In 1868 Fort Concho stood on the edge of civilization. Its first chaplain arrived while foundations for many of the post buildings were still being laid. Originally assigned to Fort Chadbourne, Thaddeus McFalls followed the Fourth Cavalry to Fort Concho. The Presbyterian minister from Pennsylvania had served as a hospital chaplain during the Civil War, when he contracted a case of typhoid fever from which he never completely recovered. By February 1869 his illness was serious enough for Doctor Notson to place him on extended sick leave and send him back to Washington, D.C., for recovery.[89]

Norman Badger, the first active chaplain at Fort Concho. Badger conducted services in a hospital ward, a barracks mess-room and even a tent erected on Officers' Row in addition to providing chapel for civilians across the river. *Courtesy Fort Concho Library and Archives.*

This left the growing post with no active chaplain during much of its construction phase. The army did employ a civilian school-master, yet the War Department made no move to replace McFalls while he was on the sick list. Finally, in 1871, McFalls was declared unfit for duty and the Rev. Norman Badger was assigned as his replacement. Born in Massachusetts in 1812, Badger graduated from the theological seminary at Kenyon College in Gambier, Ohio, and was ordained in the Episcopal Church in 1837. He served at several Episcopal parishes in Ohio before returning to Kenyon in 1840 as principal of Milnor Hall Preparatory School.[90]

In March 1864, with Civil War casualties mounting, the forty-six-year-old Badger applied for duty as an army hospital chaplain. The War Department assigned Chaplain Badger to the hospital at Jeffersonville, Indiana. In 1865 he mustered out of hospital service and became post chaplain for Taylor Barracks in Louisville, Kentucky. While there, Badger engaged in missionary work among the poor communities of Louisville, both black and white. His colleagues described him as "an ardent and enthusiastic worker for Christ." Badger also studied the army's enlistment system and made suggestions to the Adjutant General's office for reforms. His proposals included moral and educational requirements for promotion, continuing education while in service, and withholding a portion of each enlisted man's pay until the expiration of his term of service.[91]

On March 20, 1871, Norman Badger received orders to report to Fort Concho as post chaplain. He arrived on Sunday, April 9, to find the post still in the process of construction. Doctor Notson provided one of the hospital wards for worship services the following two Sundays. On the last Sunday of April Badger ventured across the river to begin his missionary work among the rough citizens of Saint Angela.[92]

The remote frontier outpost presented Chaplain Badger with a tremendous challenge. During his first month on duty, Badger took over the post school, established regular hospital and barracks visits, and began efforts to create a library. The chaplain continued to preach on Sunday afternoons to the local citizens across the river and held services for the black troops in their quarters on Sunday evenings. He also planted a post garden on ten acres leased from nearby Bismark Farm. In 1871 Badger's garden provided "almost daily supplies" to the often undernourished soldiers of "lettuce, beans, corn, squashes, cantelopes, watermellons and a small supply of okra, peas and potatoes."[93]

In November, Badger brought his wife and two of his daughters, Mahala and Sallie, to Fort Concho. With his family to support him, the chaplain began conducting worship services "of a more social character" on Sunday evenings in his quarters. He expanded the post school to include classes for officers' children during the week and for the black enlisted men at night. Badger conducted services in a hospital ward, a barracks mess-room, vacant officers' quarters, and even a tent erected on Officers' Row when quarters were full. During thunderstorms, duststorms, or high winds, the "old tent" became unusable and services sometimes had to be cancelled.[94]

Although his pleas for a permanent chapel and schoolroom went unheeded, Badger did succeed in establishing a post library. In the fall of 1873 the chaplain ordered four hundred dollars worth of literary, historical, and reference works. Beginning with 292 volumes, the library grew to include more than 720 books and a selection of magazines and newspapers by the end of 1875. Temporarily housed in the barracks room that also served as a chapel, in 1876 the library moved to a permanent reading room in the recently constructed headquarters building.[95]

In 1875 Norman Badger presided at the wedding of his daughter, Mahala, known as Haidie, to Lt. Levi P. Hunt of the Tenth Cavalry. The post still lacked a chapel, and Badger began to mention this "great want" in his monthly reports. In early 1876 he assisted black soldiers of the Tenth Cavalry in erecting a rough chapel made of wooden pickets plastered with mud and lined with flour bags saved from the post bakery. Badger reported that the troopers carried out the project "at their own expense, in despair of having a chapel and school house furnished by the government."[96] The little picket chapel proved to be Norman Badger's final project as chaplain at Fort Concho. His health and eyesight had been deteriorating since the fall of 1875. In April 1876 he requested transfer to a northern post in hopes of recovery. While awaiting the army's reply, Badger grew progressively worse, experiencing shortness of breath, ulcers on his tongue, and swelling in his lower joints. By the time a leave of absence was granted and transportation procured, his condition had become so poor he could not be moved. The frontier missionary died at Fort Concho on June 3, 1876.[97]

The chaplaincy of Norman Badger had a marked effect on the development of Fort Concho, yet it was up to his successor, the Rev. George Ward Dunbar, to complete the moral and educational work begun. The former rector of Christ Episcopal Church in Janesville, Wisconsin, arrived at Fort Concho on October 21, 1876, with his wife and two children. Observing the newest member of his staff, Colonel Grierson commented, "The Chaplain takes hold of matters as if he was determined to put forth his very best endeavor to make himself useful in every possible way and I am rather inclined to think he will be successful." The Dunbar family soon became close friends of the Griersons and the colonel assisted Dunbar's effort to continue a strong chaplaincy.[98]

On Sunday evenings Dunbar preached regularly to the black troopers in their mud and picket chapel. He reestablished the post

garden and conscientious-
ly performed the addi-
tional duties of post
librarian, bakery supervisor, and treasurer. In 1880
he even served briefly as
garrison postmaster. As
bakery supervisor, he
claimed, "Our bread is
just as good as bread any-
where. I have to be partic-
ular about that."[99]

In February 1879
workmen completed the
last permanent building
at Fort Concho on a
foundation originally
laid as the kitchen for a
new set of officers' quarters. Located at the end
of Officers' Row near the

Chaplain George W. Dunbar succeeded in having the last structure built at Fort Concho designated as a chapel and schoolhouse. *Courtesy
Fort Concho Library and Archives.*

hospital, the new structure was designated a schoolhouse and
chapel on February 22. The final work of Norman Badger had
been completed even after his death. With the new chapel in use,
Dunbar reported that services were "packed at night, many leaving for lack of room." The chaplain attempted to offer more
opportunities for worship, but in the summer of 1879 he suffered
from heat exhaustion. After that, some weeks he proved unable
to preach and on occasion he even experienced fainting spells. In
1880 he requested and received a leave of absence. Although
Dunbar recovered from his illness in the cooler climate of
Wisconsin, he did not return to Texas. A new regimental chaplain had been appointed to the Tenth Cavalry at Fort Concho,
eliminating the need for a separate post chaplain.[100]

The Tenth Cavalry chaplain, Francis H. Weaver, was the last
army chaplain to serve at Fort Concho. An Evangelical
Lutheran pastor who had served as an enlisted man during the

SCHOOLHOUSE/CHAPEL

Begun November 1878, this structure was built over a basement that was to be the kitchen section of a new officers' quarters. Lacking sufficient funding to complete the officers' quarters, the post set this space aside for education and religious services, which had previously drifted about the post in search of a home. The schoolhouse/chapel was dedicated February 22, 1879, and was declared the "best furnished room in the post." This marked the end of the twelve-year building period at Fort Concho. After the post was abandoned, this small structure served as a civilian school and later as a modest home. It became part of the Fort Concho Museum in 1946, courtesy of the San Angelo Jaycees, who renovated the facility. Additional restoration efforts over the next thirty years brought it to its current appearance. Since 1976 the building has housed "Frontier School," an 1880s-style school program for fourth graders.

Civil War, Chaplain Weaver arrived at the post on July 20, 1880. He immediately inherited the additional duties of post treasurer, gardener, and librarian. Weaver enjoyed music and encouraged singing in his Sunday school classes. In April 1881 he ordered four dozen gospel hymnbooks for the chapel. His worship services grew steadily in attendance. In a paper written to the chaplain service, he expressed the belief that "more persons proportionately attend service in the military than in civilian life."[101]

In 1882, when the Tenth Cavalry headquarters moved to Fort Davis, Weaver followed. Once again, Fort Concho was left without chaplain service, yet this time the War Department assigned no replacement. The missionary efforts of men like Norman Badger and George Dunbar had taken effect. In the once rough and violent community of San Angelo, citizens organized a Union Sunday School in 1878, established Catholic and Methodist congregations, and opened the first public school. Army regulations only provided for chaplains to those areas "most destitute of instruction" and by 1882 Fort Concho no longer qualified.[102]

Another civilizing influence in the frontier army was the post surgeon. Army surgeons and assistants were usually assigned to each outpost. The first surgeon at Fort Concho, Conrad C. Dumreicher, reported for duty at the end of 1867, when the soldiers still lived in tents. His assistant, William M. Notson, who became one of the most notable post surgeons in Fort Concho's history, arrived in January 1868. Notson was born in Philadelphia, Pennsylvania, in 1836 and graduated from medical school in 1858. He served as an army surgeon during the Civil War. At Fort Concho he settled his family into tent quarters with a large hospital tent for his surgery. By November 1868, "the hospital tents, being in a delapidated condition," Notson moved his patients into the

Dr. William Notson, the post surgeon at Fort Concho during most of its construction phase. *Courtesy Fort Concho Library and Archives.*

only finished ward of the hospital building. While workmen continued construction on the hospital, he worked, despite a shortage of medicines, to provide proper care for the sick and wounded.[103]

Notson conducted sick call every morning before breakfast. After the garrison assembled for their duties, he would examine those confined to quarters and visit the hospital wards. Common ailments among the soldiers included diarrhea, constipation, various fevers or inflammations, and venereal diseases. Later in the day Notson inspected the post and commissary supplies and recommended ways to improve sanitation. Sanitary measures proved vital to the continued existence of the post. In the first three and a half years of active service at Fort Concho, only six soldiers died of

POST HOSPITAL

Truly the most impressive structure on post, then and now, the post hospital was constructed over a two-year period between 1868 and 1870, following the same set of plans that created the Fort Richardson facility. As the only medical care facility for thousands of square miles, the army medical staff and their civilian assistants rarely lacked work. A poor supply network, lack of modern medical knowledge, and generally unsanitary conditions made their challenges even greater. After the military period, the hospital became a rooming house and storage facility. According to local lore, it was struck by lightning and burned to the ground in 1911. In the mid-1980s, the whole building was reconstructed on its original site, thanks to several years of archeological work and study. Today the post hospital has a period medical ward on the north side, general medical exhibits in the central section, and a school library in the south ward. The Fort Concho Elementary School, formerly located on the parade field, was relocated to a site adjacent to the post hospital as part of a $1.6 million reconstruction/restoration plan.

gunshot wounds. During the same period, five died from diarrhea and dysentery and eight from typhoid fever. It appeared that army rations and an often-contaminated water supply were as likely a cause of death as wounds received in an Indian attack.[104]

Doctor Notson and his successors kept a complete record of Fort Concho's development in the post medical history. In April 1870 Notson recorded the wedding of Lt. Byron Dawson to Jennie Caldwell as the first to take place on the post. He had already noted in June 1869 "the first death in an officer's family," his own infant son, Otis Rockwell Notson. Unfortunately, his was not the only loss in an officer's family. On September 9, 1878, the medical history included the death from typhoid fever of thirteen-year-old Edith Grierson, only daughter of post commander Benjamin Grierson. In March 1871 Notson listed Abijah Bayless of Bismark Farm as the first local resident to die of natural causes in the post hospital. Bayless proved to be only one of many local farmers, ranchers, and businessmen who came to Fort Concho for medical treatment. In an area devoid of even the most basic medical facility for civilians, Notson insisted, "humanity and custom, compels

The Fort Concho hospital, completed in 1870, provided the only medical care facility over thousands of square miles in West Texas. *Courtesy Fort Concho Library and Archives.*

the Medical officer, not only to exert his professional ability, but to open his hospital for their care."[105]

In addition to treating soldiers and civilians, the post surgeon often performed duties as post treasurer, librarian, and weatherman. Throughout the history of Fort Concho, the medical officer recorded monthly high and low temperatures, prevailing winds, and rainfall. Average monthly rainfall recorded at Fort Concho for 1870 to 1878 was only 2.01 inches, yet in 1882 the monthly average was 3.51 inches and the nearby town of Benficklin washed away. Post surgeons noted many extremes of weather on the West Texas frontier, including floods, droughts, dust storms, and "northers." With a responsibility for sanitation in addition to all those other duties, the Fort Concho hospital was often more than one doctor could manage. The surgeon had one or more assistants during most of the post's history.[106] When military doctors were unavailable as assistants, the army hired civilians as contract surgeons. One of the most significant contract surgeons at Fort Concho was Samuel L. S. Smith. Born in Louisville, Kentucky, in 1844, Smith reported for duty at the outpost on the Conchos in March 1878. He spent much of his time tending the troops at subposts, including Camp Charlotte and Grierson's Springs. In the summer of 1878 Smith detected an outbreak of scurvy among the patrols in the Guadalupe Mountains. Using available

The Jackson family sitting in front of the post surgeon's quarters at Fort Concho. *Courtesy Fort Concho Library and Archives.*

resources, he treated the problem by having soldiers gather aloe plants and prepare them with salt and pepper. Doctor Smith left the army medical service in 1881, but he chose to remain in the growing community of San Angelo. He became the first city physician and in 1910 helped bring the first civilian hospital to San Angelo.[107]

Also important to the post and settlement of the area around Fort Concho was the post trader or sutler. The government contracted with traders at each post to provide soldiers with a general store, which sometimes contained a bar, game room, and post office. The first trader at Fort Concho was James Trainer, an Irishman who came to Texas from New York following the Civil War. By the time Doctor Notson arrived in 1868, Trainer had already opened a sutler's store made of pickets, the first permanent building on post. He also served as the first postmaster at Fort Concho. Hoping to expand his business, Trainer purchased land west of the fort and in 1870 erected a stone structure. Trainer continued to supply the soldiers from that store, even during periods when he was not the official post trader, until September 1873.[108]

After Trainer, the sutler's contract passed through several hands and settled on William S. Veck. A native of New Jersey, Veck had come to Fort Concho as a teamster for the army and opened a store in the new town of Saint Angela. In 1875 he was appointed as a commissioner to organize Tom Green County. Veck served as postmaster and later opened the first bank in San Angelo. His ventures had a profound effect on the development of San Angelo, but his contract as post trader lasted only a brief period. In 1876 another of the county commissioners, James L. Millspaugh, became post trader at Fort Concho.[109] Described as "a small, dynamic, swashbuckling New Yorker," Millspaugh was a land promoter who had helped lay out the San Angelo townsite. He held the position of sutler until 1881. In 1884 he opened an ice factory in San Angelo, described by Captain Wedemeyer as "one of the notable signs of advancing civilization." Millspaugh also operated the first water works and worked to bring the railroad through town in 1888.[110]

As much as any officer or soldier, the chaplains, surgeons, and sutlers exemplified the rugged spirit of the frontier army. They survived the harsh environment of life at a remote outpost and tried to make it a little more civilized. In doing so, each of them had a marked effect on the daily life of Fort Concho and the developing community of San Angelo.

6.
THE LAST BUGLE CALL:
ABANDONING FORT CONCHO

ON JANUARY 27, 1881, A COMPANY of Texas Rangers under Capt. George Baylor rode into the Sierra Diablo and engaged and defeated the remnants of Victorio's Apache band in the last Indian battle fought in the state of Texas. As the Apaches moved further west into New Mexico and Arizona territories, the army followed. The Tenth Cavalry began its westward trek in 1882 when their headquarters transferred to Fort Davis in the trans–Pecos region. The War Department was not prepared to abandon Fort Concho in 1882. In August of that year the outpost on the Conchos became headquarters for the Sixteenth U.S. Infantry.[111]

Lt. Col. Alfred L. Hough arrived with the regimental headquarters staff only days after a flood had destroyed the county seat at Benficklin and badly damaged areas of San Angelo. Soldiers of the Sixteenth spent their first week on duty at Fort Concho providing rations, shelter, and medical care for the survivors. Gradually life in town returned to normal, while the Sixteenth Infantry established a daily routine on post. The army's assistance in combating local disasters such as the flood and several fires brought about a marked improvement in the previously strained relations between Fort Concho and San Angelo.[112]

As the new seat of Tom Green County prospered, the military post began to decline. Plastering in many of the buildings cracked and fell, while drainage became so poor that Surgeon John Lauderdale reported, "during a rain storm the roads and walks are but little better than water ways." In 1888 the last post surgeon,

Construction on the First National Bank demonstrates the growing prosperity of San Angelo as the new county seat. *Courtesy Fort Concho Library and Archives.*

Charles Gandy, described Fort Concho's condition as one of "general dilapidation." Capt. William George Wedemeyer of the Sixteenth Infantry agreed. The German immigrant and Civil War veteran lamented the uselessness of requiring scouting expeditions on plains now crossed by a network of barbed wire fences. Laws prevented the army from cutting through these private fences, so by the mid-1880s soldiers from Fort Concho could only patrol along public roads, where there was little need for armed troops. The wide-open stretches of Texas's South Plains had all but disappeared.[113]

In February 1887 the headquarters of the Sixteenth Infantry moved west to Fort Bliss. Many posts in the old frontier line of defense, such as Fort Griffin, had already been abandoned. By 1887 even Fort Davis was being considered for closure. Wedemeyer firmly believed that Fort Concho had been of little use in recent years and would be abandoned as soon as construction on the new barracks in San Antonio was completed. Others insisted that the

A view of the growing community of San Angelo with Fort Concho visible in the distance. *Courtesy Fort Concho Library and Archives.*

The John H. Fitzpatrick building in downtown San Angelo during the fort's active period. Note the soldier in the lower right corner. *Courtesy Fort Concho Library and Archives.*

post would close when the railroad reached San Angelo. In the spring of 1888, Fort Concho witnessed a gathering of cavalry for the last time. Under the supervision of Lt. Col. John K. Mizner, the Eighth Cavalry assembled from various posts throughout Texas. In June they rode north from Fort Concho on a 1,500-mile trek to their new post at Fort Meade, Dakota Territory. Their departure left only one company of the Nineteenth Infantry to man the Concho garrison.[114]

The Santa Fe railroad entered San Angelo on September 17, 1888. Local

Fort Concho stands abandoned after the last troops left in June 1889. *Courtesy Fort Concho Library and Archives.*

citizens, realizing that Fort Concho would soon be abandoned, appealed to the federal government for a permanent military installation, possibly using the post as a sanitarium "for the recuperation of troops." Their efforts met with no success. In June 1889, after almost twenty-two years of active service, federal troops left Fort Concho for the last time. Company K of the Nineteenth Infantry fired the final salute and lowered the flag on June 20. Early the next morning they marched away, leaving only Lt. Woodbridge Geary, the quartermaster, to settle accounts. The people of San Angelo said "a regretful farewell" as the soldiers' footsteps faded and the post stood empty.[115]

In more than twenty years of federal service Fort Concho had been home to companies of fifteen regiments in the Regular Army. The post provided a focal point for major campaigns against the Comanches, Kiowas, and Apaches. Patrols from Fort Concho charted vast areas of West Texas and provided a climate for settlement on the Texas frontier. When the army left in 1889, a collection of

LIVING HISTORY

As Fort Concho continued to restore the site's buildings and grounds, it became clear that living history presentations would enhance the daily interpretation, tours, and ongoing special events. In 1982 six fort staff and board members spent a week in a living history training camp courtesy of the National Park Service at Fort Davis, Texas. By the end of that year Fort Concho had created a program to portray the Sixteenth Infantry stationed at the post in the early 1880s. A cavalry program soon followed. An officers' wives and laundresses unit, an artillery program, and a unit to interpret the buffalo soldiers were all created within a decade. A new Living History Stables facility will be completed in late 2005, providing new space for horses, mules, and the fort's wagon units. During an average year the fort's "troops" visit many cities, festivals, and area forts while covering several dozen programs, monthly practices, and special events in San Angelo and at Fort Concho.

sturdy limestone buildings remained at the old outpost. Some of them became residences for the citizens of San Angelo, while others, left vacant, began to deteriorate. Around 1905 the Concho Realty Company was formed to buy and sell many of the surviving structures to private citizens. Then, in 1929, Ginevra Wood Carson purchased the Fort Concho headquarters building for her newly established West Texas Museum. Over the next two decades Mrs. Carson continued to expand her efforts with the establishment of the Fort Concho Museum Board to acquire and restore buildings at the old fort. The city of San Angelo began to operate the facility in 1935, developing a plan to obtain and preserve the remaining post structures. In 1961 the Fort Concho Museum became a National Historic Landmark.[116] Today Fort Concho stands restored as a memorial to all the peoples who struggled to survive on the plateau where the rivers join.

NOTES

[1] Nancy P. Hickerson, *The Jumanos: Hunters and Traders of the South Plains* (Austin: University of Texas Press, 1994), 9–12, 88–102, 110–114, 215–216; Roy Carpenter, "Early Trails," *Fort Concho Report*, 17 (Spring, 1985), 2.

[2] J. Evetts Haley, *Fort Concho and the Texas Frontier* (San Angelo: *San Angelo Standard-Times*, 1952), 1–5, 64–65, 82–87; Carpenter, "Early Trails," 4–6.

[3] Haley, *Fort Concho and the Texas Frontier*, 104–105, 122–125; James T. Matthews, "Major's Confederate Cavalry Brigade" (M.A. thesis: Texas Tech University, 1991), 70–71; Carpenter, "Early Trails," 8.

[4] Lt. Peter M. Boehm to Lt. Charles A. Vernon, July 19, 1867, Records of the Headquarters, Fort Concho, Texas, Records of United States Army Continental Commands, 1821–1928, RG 393 (National Archives).

[5] Capt. George G. Huntt to Lt. Alexander H. M. Taylor, Sept. 28, 1867, Records of the Headquarters, Fort Concho, Texas, RG 393.

[6] Captain Huntt to Capt. James G. C. Lee, Nov. 17, 1867 and Captain Huntt to the Adjutant General, United States Army, Dec. 26, 1867, Records of the Headquarters, Fort Concho, Texas, RG 393.

[7] Captain Huntt to Maj. John P. Hatch, Jan. 18, 1868, Records of the Headquarters, Fort Concho, Texas, RG 393; William N. Notson, Report for January 1869, Medical History of Post, Fort Concho, RG 94 (National Archives).

[8] Lieutenant Vernon to Captain Thompson, Aug. 15, 1867, and Captain Huntt to Lt. Wirt Davis, Aug. 15, 1867, Records of the Headquarters, Fort Concho, RG 393.

[9] Captain Huntt to Major Hatch, Jan. 18, 1868, and Maj. George C. Cram to Lt. Charles E. Morse, Apr. 8, 1868, Records of the Headquarters, Fort Concho, RG 393.

[10] Lieutenant Davis to Capt. David W. Porter, Apr. 11, Apr. 27, and Aug. 7, 1868, and Maj. George Cram to Colonel Hatch, May 9 and 25, 1868, Records of the Headquarters, Fort Concho, RG 393; Notson, Report for January 1869, Medical History of Post, Fort Concho, RG 94; Roy Eugene Graham, "Federal Fort Architecture in Texas during the Nineteenth Century," *Southwestern Historical Quarterly*, 74 (Oct., 1970), 178–181; Donald W. Whisenhunt, "Fort Richardson: Frontier Post in Northwest Texas, 1867–1878" (M.A. thesis: Texas Tech University, 1962), 12–13, 20; Bill Green, *The Dancing Was Lively: Fort Concho, Texas: A Social History, 1867 to 1882* (San Angelo: Fort Concho Sketches Publishing, 1974), 11–12.

[11] United States Ninth Census (1870), Bexar County, Texas, Population

Schedules, Fort Concho; File on Joseph Rendlebrock, Military History Collection (Fort Concho Library and Archives); Robert G. Carter, *On the Border With Mackenzie* (New York: Antiquarian Press, Ltd., 1961), 40–41.

[12] Maj. George A. Gordon to Assistant Adjutant General, Fifth Military District, Sept. 8, 1868; Report of Buildings at Fort Concho, Feb. 1, 1885, Records of the Headquarters, Fort Concho, RG 393.

[13] Record of Civilian Employees, Miscellaneous Records, Fort Concho, RG 393.

[14] Capt. George H. Gamble to Assistant Adjutant General, Fifth Military District, June 11, 1869, Records of the Headquarters, Fort Concho, RG 393; Notson, Report for August 1869, Medical History of Post, Fort Concho, RG 94.

[15] Notson, Report for October 1869, Medical History of Post, Fort Concho, RG 94; Report of Buildings at Fort Concho, Feb. 1, 1885, Records of the Headquarters, Fort Concho, RG 393.

[16] Barbara E. Fisher, "Forrestine Cooper Hooker's Notes and Memoirs on Army Life in the West, 1871–1876" (M.A. thesis: University of Arizona, 1963), 113; Notson, Report for January 1870, Medical History of Post, Fort Concho, RG 94.

[17] Notson, Reports for July, August, and September 1870, Medical History of Post, Fort Concho, RG 94.

[18] Notson, Reports for March, April, July and October 1871, Medical History of Post, Fort Concho, RG 94.

[19] Notson, Report for February 1872, Medical History of Post, Fort Concho, RG 94; Record of Civilian Employees, Miscellaneous Records, Fort Concho, RG 393.

[20] Notson, Report for March 1872, Medical History of Post, Fort Concho, RG 94.

[21] Norman Badger, Report for August 1874, Chaplain's Report, Fort Concho, RG 94; William H. and Shirley A. Leckie, *Unlikely Warriors: General Benjamin Grierson and His Family* (Norman: University of Oklahoma Press, 1984), 180, 224–225.

[22] George Dunbar, Chaplain's Report for January 1879, Fort Concho, RG 94; Benjamin Grierson to Alice Grierson, July 1, 1879, Grierson Collection, Southwest Collection (Texas Tech University, Lubbock).

[23] William Buchanon, Reports for 1883, Medical History of Post, Fort Concho, RG 94.

[24] *San Antonio Express*, May 11, 1877.

[25] Notson, Reports for July, August and September 1870 and April 1871, Medical History of Post, Fort Concho, RG 94; File on Subposts, Reference files (Fort Concho Library and Archives).

[26] Notson, Reports for February and July 1869 and February 1871, Medical History of Post, Fort Concho, RG 94; Ernest Wallace, *Ranald S. Mackenzie on the Texas Frontier* (Lubbock: West Texas Museum Association, 1964), 39–45.

[27] Col. R. S. Mackenzie to Assistant Adjutant General, Department of Texas, in Ernest Wallace (ed.), *Ranald S. Mackenzie's Official Correspondence Relating to Texas, 1871–1873* (Lubbock: West Texas Museum Association, 1967), 54–55; Notson, Report for March 1872, Medical History of Post, Fort Concho, RG 94; and Sgt. William Wilson, Report of Scout, Mar. 29, 1872, Records of the Headquarters, Fort Concho, RG 393.

[28] Wilson, Report of Scout, Mar. 29, 1872, Records of the Headquarters, Fort Concho, RG 393. For further information concerning Sgt. William Wilson see also Charles M. Neal Jr., *Valor across the Lone Star: The Congressional Medal of Honor in Frontier Texas* (Austin: Texas State Historical Association, 2002).

[29] Wilson, Report of Scout, Mar. 29, 1872, Records of the Headquarters, Fort Concho, RG 393; Notson, Report for March 1872, Medical History of the Post, and Norman Badger, Report for March 1872, Chaplain's Report, Fort Concho, RG 94.

[30] Maj. John P. Hatch to Gen. Gordon Granger, Mar. 31, 1872, and Hatch to Assistant Adjutant General, Department of Texas, Apr. 15, 1872, in Wallace (ed.), *Mackenzie's Official Correspondence, 1871–1873*, 45–48.

[31] Hatch to Assistant Adjutant General, Department of Texas, Apr. 15, 1872, and Hatch to Granger, Apr. 16, 1872, in Wallace (ed.), *Mackenzie's Official Correspondence, 1871–1873*, 47–51; Hatch to Gen. Eli Long, June 13, 1872 (Fort Concho Library and Archives).

[32] Hatch to Assistant Adjutant General, Department of Texas, May 16, 1872, and Capt. Napoleon B. McLaughlin, Report of Scout, May 15, 1872, in Wallace (ed.), *Mackenzie's Official Correspondence, 1871–1873*, 63–69; Notson, Report for May 1872, Medical History of the Post, Fort Concho, RG 94.

[33] Notson, Reports for May and June 1872, Medical History of the Post, Fort Concho, RG 94; Gen. Christopher C. Augur, Special Orders no. 102, Department of Texas, May 31, 1872, and Hatch to Assistant Adjutant General, Department of Texas, June 17, 1872, in Wallace (ed.), *Mackenzie's Official Correspondence, 1871–1873*, 71–73.

[34] McLaughlin, Report of Scout, July 2–14, 1872, and Mackenzie to Assistant Adjutant General, Department of Texas, Aug. 7, Aug. 15, and Sept. 3, 1872, in Wallace (ed.), *Mackenzie's Official Correspondence, 1871–1873*, 116–120, 127–130, 133–134; Wallace, *Mackenzie on the Texas Frontier*, 69–73.

[35] Mackenzie to Assistant Adjutant General, Department of Texas, Oct. 12, 1872, in Wallace (ed.), *Mackenzie's Official Correspondence, 1871–1873*, 141–142.

[36] Ibid., 142–143; Michael D. Pierce, *The Most Promising Young Officer: A Life of Ranald Slidell Mackenzie* (Norman: University of Oklahoma Press, 1993), 116–117.

[37] Mackenzie to Assistant Adjutant General, Department of Texas, Oct. 12, 1872, with endorsements by Gen. Philip H. Sheridan and Gen. William T. Sherman, in Wallace (ed.), *Mackenzie's Official Correspondence, 1871–1873*, 143–147.

[38] Mackenzie to Assistant Adjutant General, Department of Texas, Oct. 12, 1872, with endorsement by General Augur, Oct. 25, 1872, in Wallace (ed.), *Mackenzie's Official Correspondence, 1871–1873*, 142–145; Regimental Return, Fourth U. S. Cavalry, October 1872, RG 94; Wayne Daniel and Carol Schmidt (eds.), "Wild as Coyotes: Indian Prisoners at Fort Concho, 1872–73," *Fort Concho Report*, 17 (Summer, 1985), 21–25.

[39] Daniel and Schmidt (eds.), "Wild as Coyotes," 25–27; Post Return, Fort Concho, Texas, May 1873, RG 94; Carter, *On the Border*, 390–391. For additional information on Indian captives in Texas see Scott Zesch, *The Captured: A True Story of Indian Abduction on the Texas Frontier* (New York: St. Martin's Press, 2004).

[40] Post Return, Fort Concho, Texas, March 1873, RG 94; Wallace, *Mackenzie on the Texas Frontier*, 92–95.

[41] Wallace, *Mackenzie on the Texas Frontier*, 96–100; Mackenzie to Assistant Adjutant General, Department of Texas, May 23, 1873, in Wallace (ed.), *Mackenzie's Official Correspondence, 1871–1873*, 168, 170; Pierce, *Most Promising Young Officer*, 124–129.

[42] Mackenzie to Assistant Adjutant General, Department of Texas, May 23, 1873, in Wallace (ed.), *Mackenzie's Official Correspondence, 1871–1873*, 168–170; Francis B. Heitman, *Historical Record and Dictionary of the United States Army from its Organization, September 29, 1789, to March 2, 1903* (Washington, D.C.: Government Printing Office, 1903), 674–675; Pierce, *Most Promising Young Officer*, 129–130.

[43] Wallace, *Mackenzie on the Texas Frontier*, 102–110; Pierce, *Most Promising Young Officer*, 131–140.

[44] Special Orders no. 113, Department of Texas, July 23, 1874, in Ernest Wallace (ed.), *Ranald S. Mackenzie's Official Correspondence Relating to Texas, 1873–1879* (Lubbock: West Texas Museum Association, 1968), 79; Wallace, *Mackenzie on the Texas Frontier*, 120–125.

[45] Mackenzie's Journal of Campaign: Part I, Sept. 20–29, 1874; Mackenzie to Assistant Adjutant General, Department of Texas, Sept. 19, 1874; Mackenzie's Expedition as Described by a Special Correspondent to the *New York Herald*, Sept. 29, 1874, in Wallace (ed.), *Mackenzie's Official Correspondence, 1873–1879*, 119–122, 93, 112–115.

[46] Mackenzie's Expedition as Described by a Special Correspondent to the *New York Herald*, Sept. 29, 1874; Mackenzie's Journal of Campaign: Part I, Sept. 20–29, 1874; Mackenzie to Assistant Adjutant General, Department of Texas, Oct. 1, 1874, in Wallace (ed.), *Mackenzie's Official Correspondence, 1873–1879*, 116–117, 122–125.

[47] Pierce, *Most Promising Young Officer*, 157–163.

[48] Elizabeth K. Oaks, "Benjamin H. Grierson: Reluctant Horse Soldier and Gentle Raider" (M.A. thesis: Mississippi State University, 1981), 4–12, 22–24, 109; United States Tenth Census (1880), Tom Green County, Texas, Population Schedules, Fort Concho.

[49] Col. Benjamin H. Grierson to Capt. Nicholas Nolan, July 4, 1877, RG 98 (National Archives); Joseph H. King, "Brief Account of the Sufferings of a Detachment of United States Cavalry From Deprivation of Water," *The American Journal of the Medical Sciences*, 75 (1878), 405–406; Haley, *Fort Concho and the Texas Frontier*, 246–250.

[50] King, "Sufferings of a Detachment of Cavalry," 406–408; Haley, *Fort Concho and the Texas Frontier*, 257–259.

[51] General Orders no. 2, Department of Texas, Jan. 22, 1878, RG 98.

[52] Lt. Robert H. Swisher to Commanding Officer, Company C, Tenth Cavalry, Mar. 28, 1878, U.S. Army, Continental Commands, 1821–1920, District of the Pecos Records, 1878–1881, RG 393; Report of Capt. Thomas C. Lebo to Post Adjutant, Fort Davis, Feb. 16, 1879, RG 98; Document file for "Fort Davis—Subposts" (Fort Davis Archives).

[53] John Neilson, "'I Long to Return to Fort Concho': Acting Assistant Surgeon Samuel Smith's Letters From the Texas Military Frontier, 1878–1879," *Military History of the West*, 24 (Fall, 1994), 184; Colonel Grierson to Assistant Adjutant

General, Department of Texas, Aug. 2, 1878; Lieutenant Swisher to Lt. Mason M. Maxon, May 19, 1878; Special Orders no. 8, District of the Pecos, July 31, 1878, District of the Pecos Records, RG 393.

[54] Report of Colonel Grierson to Assistant Adjutant General, Department of Texas, Dec. 31, 1879; Colonel Grierson to Assistant Adjutant General, Department of Texas, Feb. 15, 1880, District of the Pecos Records, RG 393.

[55] Dan L. Thrapp, *Victorio and the Mimbres Apaches* (Norman: University of Oklahoma Press, 1974), 3–5, 188–193, 214–219; *New York Times*, Nov. 28, 1880.

[56] Colonel Grierson to Assistant Adjutant General, Department of Texas, May 21, 1880, District of the Pecos Records, RG 393.

[57] Ibid.; Report of Capt. Louis H. Carpenter to Assistant Adjutant General, Department of Texas, Dec. 9, 1880, District of the Pecos Records, RG 393.

[58] Lieutenant Swisher to Company M, Tenth Cavalry, May 25, 1880; Report of Capt. Louis H. Carpenter to Assistant Adjutant General, Department of Texas, Dec. 9, 1880; Special Orders no. 5, Mar. 2, 1880, District of the Pecos Records, RG 393.

[59] Report of Colonel Grierson to Assistant Adjutant General, Department of Texas, Dec. 31, 1880; Special Orders no. 17, District of the Pecos, June 27, 1880, District of the Pecos Records, RG 393.

[60] General Orders no. 3, District of the Pecos, July 9, 1880; Special Orders no. 27, District of the Pecos, Aug. 25, 1880; Colonel Grierson to Commanding Officer, Fort Bliss, July 18, 1880; Col. Adolfo Valle to Colonel Grierson, July 25, 1880, telegram, District of the Pecos Records, RG 393.

[61] Report of Colonel Grierson to Assistant Adjutant General, Department of Texas, Sept. 20, 1880, District of the Pecos Records, RG 393; Robert K. Grierson, "Journal Kept on the Victorio Campaign in 1880," typescript (Fort Concho Library and Archives).

[62] Report of Colonel Grierson to Assistant Adjutant General, Department of Texas, Sept. 20, 1880, and Colonel Grierson to Captain Carpenter, July 30, 1880, District of the Pecos Records, RG 393.

[63] R. Grierson, "Journal of the Victorio Campaign"; Report of Colonel Grierson to Assistant Adjutant General, Department of Texas, Sept. 20, 1880; Report of Captain Carpenter to Assistant Adjutant General, Department of Texas, Dec. 9, 1880, District of the Pecos Records, RG 393.

[64] Ibid.

[65] Harold Ray Sayre, *Warriors of Color* (Fort Davis: H. R. Sayre, 1975), 109.

[66] Telegram from Joaquim Terrazas to Col. George P. Buell, Oct. 18, 1880; Reports of Colonel Grierson to Assistant Adjutant General, Department of Texas, Sept. 20, 1880, and Dec. 31, 1880; Lt. William Beck to Capt. William B. Kennedy, Aug. 11, 1880; Beck to Commanding Officer, Fort Quitman, Aug. 18, 1880, District of the Pecos Records, RG 393.

[67] General Orders no. 1, District of the Pecos, Feb. 7, 1881, District of the Pecos Records, RG 393; Regimental Return, Tenth U.S. Cavalry, July 1882, RG 94.

[68] Neilson, "'I Long to Return to Fort Concho,'" 149; Notson, Buchanon, and King, Surgeon's Reports for 1870, 1873 and 1878, Medical History of Post, Fort Concho, RG 94. A good source of information concerning army posts in Texas and

the units stationed at each one is Thomas T. Smith, *The Old Army in Texas: A Research Guide to the U.S. Army in Nineteenth-Century Texas* (Austin: Texas State Historical Association, 1999).

[69] Buchanon and J. V. DeHanne, Surgeon's Reports for 1875 and 1878, Medical History of Post; Badger, Chaplain's Reports for 1871, Fort Concho, RG 94.

[70] Neilson, "'I Long to Return to Fort Concho,'" 177; W. F. Carter, Buchanon, and DeHanne, Surgeon's Reports for 1877, 1878 and 1880, Medical History of Post, Fort Concho, RG 94.

[71] James T. Matthews, "Cavalry Traditions on the Texas Frontier," *The Permian Historical Annual*, 30 (Dec., 1990), 94–95; Carter, *On the Border*, 340–343.

[72] Carter, *On the Border*, 332–340; "Memoirs of William George Wedemeyer, U.S.A., Major, 16th Infantry, 1836–1902," II, 98, 278, 2 vols., typescript (Fort Concho Library and Archives).

[73] Fisher, "Forrestine Cooper Hooker's Memoirs," 115–116.

[74] Robert Wooster, *Soldiers, Sutlers, and Settlers: Garrison Life on the Texas Frontier* (College Station: Texas A&M University Press, 1987), 64–70.

[75] Neilson, "'I Long to Return to Fort Concho,'" 145, 167; Wedemeyer, "Memoirs," 107, 120, 126; Wooster, *Soldiers, Sutlers, and Settlers*, 106–107.

[76] United States Ninth Census (1870), Bexar County, Texas, Population Schedules, Fort Concho.

[77] United States Tenth Census (1880), Tom Green County, Texas, Population Schedules, Fort Concho.

[78] Notson, Surgeon's Reports for March, May, and November 1869 and January 1870, Medical History of Post, Fort Concho, RG 94.

[79] Wedemeyer, "Memoirs," 99, 104, 128–129.

[80] Neilson, "'I Long to Return to Fort Concho,'" 145–146; General Court Martial Orders no. 43, 1871 and General Court Martial Orders no. 38, 1883, Department of Texas, Records of the Headquarters, RG 393.

[81] Notson, Surgeon's Report for July 1871, Medical History of Post, Fort Concho, RG 94; General Court Martial Orders no. 43, 1871, General Court Martial Orders no. 38, 1883, and Circular no. 29, 1884, Department of Texas, Records of the Headquarters, RG 393.

[82] Fisher, "Forrestine Cooper Hooker's Memoirs," 113–114; Notson, Surgeon's Reports for February and September 1870, Medical History of Post, Fort Concho, RG 94.

[83] Fisher, "Forrestine Cooper Hooker's Memoirs," 114; Notson, Surgeon's Report for November 1871, Medical History of Post, Fort Concho, RG 94; Neilson, "'I Long to Return to Fort Concho,'" 146.

[84] Wedemeyer, "Memoirs," 100–101; *San Antonio Daily Express*, Jan. 21, 1881; Bruce J. Dinges, "The San Angelo Riot of 1881: A Reassessment," 4–5, paper presented at the Texas State Historical Association annual meeting, Mar. 5, 1993, copy in "Riots—Fort Concho" file (Fort Concho Library and Archives).

[85] Wedemeyer, "Memoirs," 101–102; *San Antonio Daily Express*, Feb. 11, 1881; Dinges, "The San Angelo Riot," 5–7.

[86] Wedemeyer, "Memoirs," 102–104; *San Antonio Daily Express*, Feb. 11, 1881; Dinges, "The San Angelo Riot," 7–11.

[87] Wedemeyer, "Memoirs," 103–104, 300; Dinges, "The San Angelo Riot," 10–13.

[88] Notson, Surgeon's Report for April 1871, Medical History of Post, Fort Concho, RG 94.

[89] Heitman, *Historical Register and Dictionary of the United States Army*, 665; Biographical file on Thaddeus McFalls (Fort Concho Library and Archives).

[90] Biographical file on Norman Badger, Olin Library Special Collections (Kenyon College, Gambier, Ohio).

[91] Badger File, Olin Library Special Collections; *Gambier Weekly Argus*, June 29, 1876; Badger file and letters of Norman Badger to Adjutant General, Feb. 22 and Apr. 19, 1871 (Fort Concho Library and Archives).

[92] Badger to Adjutant General, Apr. 19, 1871 (Fort Concho Library and Archives); Notson, Report for April 1871, Medical History of Post, RG 94.

[93] Norman Badger, Reports for April, May and July 1871, Chaplain's Report and Notson, Reports for April and July 1871, Medical History of Post, RG 94 (National Archives); Mary Bain Spence, "Sketches on the Early Settlement of the Concho Country," copy of unpublished paper, 1980 (Fort Concho Library and Archives).

[94] Badger, Reports for November 1871, December 1872, May and June 1873, January, March, August, and September 1874, January, May, and August 1875, and February 1876, Chaplain's Report; and Notson, Report for July 1871, Medical History of Post, RG 94.

[95] Badger, Reports for May 1873, March 1874, May 1875, and February 1876, Chaplain's Report, RG 94.

[96] Fisher, "Forrestine Cooper Hooker's Memoirs," 128; Badger, Report for February 1876, Chaplain's Report, RG 94.

[97] Badger file (Fort Concho Library and Archives); William F. Buchanon, Special Report in the Case of Norman Badger, August 1876, Medical History of Post, RG 94; Badger file, Olin Library Special Collections (Kenyon College, Gambier, Ohio).

[98] Biographical file on George W. Dunbar; Benjamin Grierson to Alice Grierson, October 1876, Addie Dunbar to Alice Grierson, Aug. 1, 1880, letters (Fort Concho Library and Archives).

[99] Dunbar file; George Dunbar to Mrs. M. J. Dunbar, Feb. 24, 1878, letter (Fort Concho Library and Archives); Dunbar, Reports for September 1877 and February 1880, Chaplain's Report, RG 94.

[100] Dunbar, Reports for March 1879 and February 1880, Chaplain's Report, RG 94; Dunbar file; George Dunbar to Adjutant General, Sept. 13, 1880, and Oct. 1, 1896, and W. P. Pence to Adjutant General, Apr. 6, 1911, letters (Fort Concho Library and Archives).

[101] Heitman, *Historical Register and Dictionary of the United States Army*, 1011; Biographical file on Francis H. Weaver (Fort Concho Library and Archives); Francis Weaver, Report for April 1881, Chaplain's Report, RG 94.

[102] Weaver file (Fort Concho Library and Archives); Rose Austin, *Early History of San Angelo* (San Angelo: Fort Concho Museum, 1950), 4–6.

[103] *San Angelo Standard-Times*, Mar. 16, 1971; Notson, Surgeon's Reports for 1869, Medical History of Post, Fort Concho, RG 94.

[104] Register of the Sick and Wounded, 1868–1887, Fort Concho and Surgeon's Reports for 1869–1872, Medical History of Post, Fort Concho, RG 94; John Neilson, "Soldiers and Surgeons: Army Medical Practice at Fort Concho, Texas, 1867–1889," *West Texas Historical Association Yearbook*, 69 (1993), 47.

[105] Notson, Surgeon's Reports for June 1869, April 1870, and March 1871, and DeHanne, Surgeon's Report for September 1878, Medical History of Post, Fort Concho, RG 94.

[106] Neilson, "'I Long to Return to Fort Concho,'" 178; Surgeon's Reports for 1869–1882, Medical History of Post, Fort Concho, RG 94.

[107] Neilson, "'I Long to Return to Fort Concho,'" 125–126, 139, 186; Neilson, "Soldiers and Surgeons," 50–51.

[108] Biographical file on James Trainer (Fort Concho Library and Archives); Notson, Surgeon's Reports for September 1870 and February 1871; Green, *The Dancing Was Lively*, 37–39.

[109] Green, *The Dancing Was Lively*, 39; Mary Bain Spence, "Sketches on the Early Settlement of the Concho Country," Apr. 19, 1960, typescript, 10–11 (Tom Green County Library, San Angelo).

[110] Spence, "Sketches of the Concho Country," 16–17; Wedemeyer, "Memoirs," 303.

[111] George W. Baylor, "The Last Fight on Texas Soil Between the Apaches and Texas Rangers," *The Texas Rangers Association*, 5 (Dec., 1905), 18–19; Post Returns, Fort Concho, Texas, July and August 1882, RG 94.

[112] Katharine T. Waring, "Ben Ficklin's Flood," *Fort Concho Report*, 14 (Fall, 1982), 3–18; John C. Neilson, "The Commanding Officers of Fort Concho: The Final Chapter, 1882–89," *Fort Concho and the South Plains Journal*, 24 (Spring, 1992), 22.

[113] John V. Lauderdale and Charles M. Gandy, Surgeon's Reports for June 1884, August 1886, June 1887, November 1888, Medical History of Post, Fort Concho, RG 94; Wedemeyer, "Memoirs," 289, 334.

[114] Wedemeyer, "Memoirs," 302; Post Returns, Fort Concho, Texas, February 1887 and May 1888, RG 94; Neilson, "Commanding Officers of Fort Concho," 31.

[115] Robert F. Bluthardt, "Prelude to Preservation: The Abandonment of Fort Concho," *Fort Concho Report*, 21 (Summer, 1989), 8–10; *San Angelo Standard*, June 22, 1889; Post Return, Fort Concho, Texas, June 1889, RG 94.

[116] Bluthardt, "Prelude to Preservation," 16–17.

INDEX

Illustrations are noted in *italics*.